FUN WITH
CHINESE CHA
The Straits Times C

Cartoonist: Tan Huay Peng

Marshall Cavendish
Editions

Published for The Straits Times
by Marshall Cavendish Editions
An imprint of Marshall Cavendish International
1 New Industrial Road, Singapore 536196

First published 1983
Reprinted 1984, 1985, 1986, 1987 (twice), 1988 (twice), 1989, 1990, 1991 (twice), 1992 (twice), 1993,
       1994 (three times), 1995 (three times), 1996, 1997, 1999, 2000, 2002, 2004, 2005, 2006

Other Marshall Cavendish Offices

Marshall Cavendish Ltd. 119 Wardour Street, London W1F 0UW, UK • Marshall Cavendish Corporation. 99 White Plains Road, Tarrytown NY 10591-9001, USA • Marshall Cavendish International (Thailand) Co Ltd. 253 Asoke, 12th Flr, Sukhumvit 21 Road, Klongtoey Nua, Wattana, Bangkok 10110, Thailand • Marshall Cavendish (Malaysia) Sdn Bhd, Times Subang, Lot 46, Subang Hi-Tech Industrial Park, Batu Tiga, 40000 Shah Alam, Selangor Darul Ehsan, Malaysia

Marshall Cavendish is a trademark of Times Publishing Limited

National Library Board Singapore Cataloguing in Publication Data

Fun with Chinese Characters.–3 / – cartoonist, Tan Huay Peng.
Singapore : Times Books International, 2002.
p.cm, – (The Straits Times collection)
First published in 1983.
ISBN-13: 978-981-232-452-8
ISBN-10: 981-232-452-6
1. Chinese characters. 2. Chinese language – Writing. I. Chen, Huoping.
II. Series: The Straits Times collection
PL1171
495.181—dc21   SLS2002034075

Printed in Malaysia by Times Offset (M) Sdn Bhd

PREFACE

Fun With Chinese Characters Volume 3 features another 140 characters which first appeared in the Straits Times Bilingual Page. They trace systematically the evolution of Chinese characters from pictographs and ideographs, introducing radical elements and compounds with the appreciative and discerning eye of a cartoonist.

This final collection in the highly popular and successful Fun With Chinese Characters Series includes an indispensable index of all the characters found in the series for easy reference.

CONTENTS 目录

1	王	wáng	27	轿	jiào	53	够	gòu	79	洗	xǐ
2	玉	yù	28	软	ruǎn	54	爹	diē	80	波	bō
3	国	guó	29	连	lián	55	外	wài	81	海	hǎi
4	现	xiàn	30	莲	lián	56	梦	mèng	82	渴	kě
5	里	lǐ	31	父	fù	57	夜	yè	83	法	fǎ
6	理	lǐ	32	巾	jīn	58	名	míng	84	林	lín
7	主	zhǔ	33	布	bù	59	铭	míng	85	枝	zhī
8	住	zhù	34	帚	zhǒu	60	怨	yuàn	86	椅	yǐ
9	全	quán	35	妇	fù	61	从	cóng	87	楼	lóu
10	痊	quán	36	帝	dì	62	行	xíng, háng	88	病	bìng
11	米	mǐ	37	带	dài	63	得	dé	89	疼	téng
12	粉	fěn	38	帽	mào	64	德	dé	90	疾	jí
13	精	jīng	39	常	cháng	65	徒	tú	91	道	dào
14	气	qì	40	帮	bāng	66	很	hěn	92	面	miàn
15	食	shí	41	衣	yí	67	街	jiē	93	瞎	xiā
16	饭	fàn	42	裤	kù	68	律	lǜ	94	睡	shuì
17	饱	bǎo	43	被	bèi	69	后	hòu	95	发	fā
18	饿	è	44	表	biǎo	70	待	dài	96	胃	wèi
19	馆	guǎn	45	片	piàn	71	功	gōng	97	思	sī
20	饮	yǐn	46	床	chuáng	72	加	jiā	98	情	qíng
21	车	chē	47	墙	qiáng	73	办	bàn	99	拜	bài
22	轰	hōng	48	将	jiāng	74	协	xié	100	放	fàng
23	库	kù	49	壮	zhuàng	75	劳	láo	101	政	zhèng
24	轮	lún	50	装	zhuāng	76	烦	fán	102	菜	cài
25	军	jūn	51	夕	xī	77	光	guàng	103	甜	tián
26	斩	zhǎn	52	多	duō	78	先	xiān	104	叫	jiào

105	听	tīng	114	娘	niáng	123	石	shí	132	士	shì
106	聋	lóng	115	妙	miào	124	仙	xiān	133	做	zuò
107	喜	xǐ	116	客	kè	125	高	gāo	134	众	zhòng
108	春	chūn	117	比	bǐ	126	京	jīng	135	价	jià
109	唱	chàng	118	背	bèi	127	空	kōng	136	话	huà
110	歌	gē	119	凶	xiōng	128	船	chuán	137	语	yǔ
111	鸣	míng	120	答	dá	129	贫	pín	138	去	qù
112	吐	tǔ	121	篮	lán	130	圆	yuán	139	回	huí
113	如	rú	122	井	jǐng	131	儿	ér	140	凸	tū
										凹	āo

WÁNG

王

king; ruler

THREE horizontal planes (三) representing heaven, man and earth, connected by a vertical structure (丨), form the character for king: 王 — the one vested with power, between heaven and earth, to rule uprightly over man. Originally 王 was a pictograph of a string of jade beads (王) which only the royalty could afford. It eventually became the symbol for king.

一 二 干 王

国王	guó wáng	king	
王朝	wáng cháo	imperial court; dynasty	
王储	wáng chǔ	crown prince	
王法	wáng fǎ	the law	
王公贵族	wáng gōng guì zú	the nobility	

王宫	wáng gōng	(imperial) palace
王牌	wáng pái	trump card
王室	wáng shì	royal family; imperial court
王位	wáng wèi	throne
王族	wáng zú	persons of royal lineage

Example:

国 王 死 后 ， 王 子 将 继 承 王 位 。

Guó wáng sǐ hòu wáng zǐ jiāng jì chéng wáng wèi

When the king dies, the prince will succeed to the throne.

1

玉 YÙ

jade; gem

三 represents 3 pieces of jade strung together as a symbol for king: 王. The dot (丶) was added to form 玉 (jade), distinguishing it from 王 (king). Highly valued as a symbol of excellence and purity, jade may be found in its crude form, hidden in rough stone. Hence the saying: "Jade which is not chiselled and polished is not an article of beauty."

一 二 干 王 玉

玉雕	yù diāo	jade carving; jade sculpture
玉皇大帝	yù huáng dà dì	the Jade Emperor (the Supreme Deity of Taoism)
玉洁冰清	yù jié bīng qīng	as pure as jade and as clean as ice
玉器	yù qì	jade article
玉色	yù sè	jade green; light bluish green
玉蜀黍	yù shǔ shǔ	maize; corn
玉兔	yù tù	the Jade Hare — the moon
玉簪	yù zān	jade hairpin

Example:

这 个 玉 雕 不 便 宜 。
Zhè ge yù diāo bù pián yi
This jade carving is not cheap.

2

国 (國)

GUÓ　country; nation

國 is composed of 囗 (boundary), 一 (land), 口 (mouth) and 戈 (spear). 國 therefore means land, people and weapons within a boundary — a country. The simplified form puts only 玉 (jade, representing king) within the boundary (囗) to produce nation: 国 . But a king needs subjects as much as subjects need food: "People are the nation's source; food is the primary need of the people."

PENG

丨 冂 冂 冃 用 国 国 国

国宾	guó bīn	state guest	国会	guó huì	parliament
国策	guó cè	national policy	国籍	guó jí	nationality
国产	guó chǎn	made in our country	国际	guó jì	international
国都	guó dū	national capital	国内市场	guó nèi shì chǎng	domestic market
国法	guó fǎ	the law of the land	国庆	guó qìng	National Day
国防	guó fáng	national defence	国事访问	guó shì fǎng wèn	state visit
国歌	guó gē	national anthem			

Example:

唱 国 歌 时 要 立 正 。

Chàng guó gē shí yào lì zhèng

Stand at attention when singing the national anthem.

现 (現)

XIÀN   appear; reveal; now

THE radical is 玉 (jade, gem) contracted to 王. The phonetic 見, representing eyes (目) of man (儿), means to see. So 现 means the sight of a sparkling gem, its appearance at that very moment; now. Appearances may be revealing or deceptive. According to the saying: "Fine words and appearance are seldom associated with virtue."

一 二 干 王 玑 玑 现 现

现场	xiàn chǎng	scene (of an incident)
现成	xiàn chéng	ready-made
现代	xiàn dài	modern times; the contemporary age
现款	xiàn kuǎn	ready money; cash
现实	xiàn shí	reality; actuality

现象	xiàn xiàng	appearance (of things); phenomenon
现有	xiàn yǒu	now available; existing
现在	xiàn zài	now; at present; today
出现	chū xiàn	appear
发现	fā xiàn	discover

Example:

她 脸 上 现 出 一 丝 笑 容 。
Tā liǎn shàng xiàn chū yī sī xiào róng
A faint smile appeared on her face.

4

LǏ   village; mile; inside

里 originally was a village made up of 田 (fields) and 土 (earth). The average length of one side, about 600 metres, became a measure of length: 里 , a Chinese mile. 里 is also the simplified form of 裏 . Here the radical for clothes (衣) is split and lined inside with the phonetic 里 to suggest inside: 裏 .

丶	冂	冋	日	旦	甲	里						

里边	lǐ bian	inside; in; within
里程	lǐ chéng	mileage; course of development
里程碑	lǐ chéng bēi	milestone
里海	Lǐ Hǎi	the Caspian Sea
里面	lǐ miàn	inside; interior
里头	lǐ tou	inside; interior

Example:

屋 子 里 面 充 满 阳 光 。
Wū zi lǐ miàn chōng mǎn yáng guāng
The house is filled with sunshine.

理 LǏ

polish;
reason;
principle

玉 (gem) is the radical, and the phonetic 里 is made up of 田 (field) and 土 (land). 理 compares the cutting of a gem to the dividing of field and land, both done according to fixed rules and principles; hence the extended meaning: reason, principle. The old saying highlights the importance of a moral standard: "A man of talent without principle is inferior to a simpleton with principle."

PENG

一 二 千 王 玗 玑 玾 珇 珅 理 理

理睬	lǐ cǎi	(usually in the negative) pay attention to; show interest in
理发	lǐ fà	haircut; hairdressing
理会	lǐ huì	understand; comprehend
理解	lǐ jiě	understand; comprehend
理科	lǐ kē	science (as a school subject)

理论	lǐ lùn	theory
理事会	lǐ shì huì	council; board of directors
理所当然	lǐ suǒ dāng rán	of course; naturally
理想	lǐ xiǎng	ideal
理性	lǐ xìng	reason
理由	lǐ yóu	reason; ground; argument
理智	lǐ zhì	reason; intellect

Example:

我 有 充 分 理 由 相 信 他 的 话 。
Wǒ yǒu chōng fèn lǐ yóu xiāng xìn tā de huà
I have every reason to believe his words.

主

ZHǓ   owner; master

主 is a pictograph of a lampstand with the flame rising above it. It symbolises a man who spreads light — a lord or master. To shed light, the master himself needs the enlightening counsel: "If you suspect a man, don't employ him; if you employ a man, don't suspect him."

| 丶 | 二 | 二 | 于 | 主 | | | | | | | |

主办	zhǔ bàn	direct; sponsor		主人	zhǔ rén	master
主持	zhǔ chí	chair (a discussion); host (a banquet)		主任	zhǔ rèn	director; chairman
主动	zhǔ dòng	initiative		主使	zhǔ shǐ	instigate; incite; abet
主队	zhǔ duì	home team; host team		主题	zhǔ tí	theme; subject; motif
主妇	zhǔ fù	housewife; hostess		主席	zhǔ xí	chairman (of a meeting)
主观	zhǔ guān	subjective		主要	zhǔ yào	main; chief; principal
主管	zhǔ guǎn	person in charge		主义	zhǔ yì	doctrine; -ism
				主意	zhǔ yì	idea; plan; decision

Example:

我 们 应 该 主 动 去 接 近 他 。
Wǒ men yīng gāi zhǔ dòng qù jiē jìn tā

We ought to take the initiative to befriend him.

住

ZHÙ

live;
reside;
stay

人 (man) is combined with 主 (master) to form 住, meaning to dwell. In ancient days, the man (人) was always master (主) of his dwelling; so the combination 住 suggests to dwell, to stay. In modern times, however, some husbands still boss the house; others house the boss.

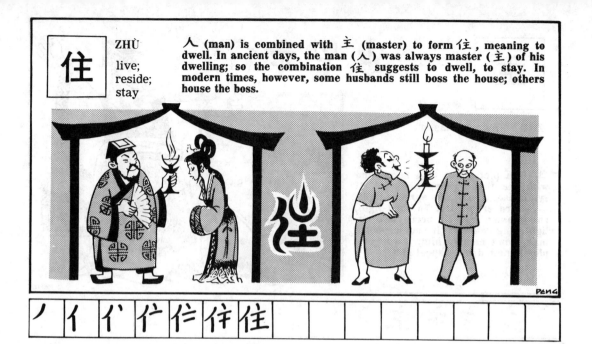

丿 亻 亻 亻 亻 住 住

住户	zhù hù	household; resident
住口	zhù kǒu	shut up; stop talking
住手	zhù shǒu	stay one's hand; stop
住宿	zhù sù	stay; put up; get accommodation
住院	zhù yuàn	be in hospital; be hospitalized
住宅	zhù zhái	residence; dwelling

Example:

他 大 部 分 时 间 在 学 校 住 宿 。

Tā dà bù fèn shí jiān zài xué xiào zhù sù

He stayed at the school most of the time.

8

QUÁN

全

complete;
perfect

THIS character was first written 全 or 仝, combining 스 (joined) with 工 (work). It means completed, i.e., the components are assembled and the work finished. However, the modern character, classified under 入 (in), could be interpreted as a jade (王 or 玉) skilfully inlaid (入), and so flawless and perfect: 全. But perfection is not always the crucial thing: "Better an imperfect jade than a perfect tile."

PENG

| ノ | 人 | 스 | 仐 | 仝 | 全 | | | | | | | |

全部	quán bù	whole; complete; total; all	全局	quán jú	overall situation
全才	quán cái	a versatile person; all-rounder	全力	quán lì	with all one's strength
全场	quán chǎng	the whole audience; all those present	全面	quán miàn	overall; comprehensive
全国性	quán guó xìng	nationwide	全年	quán nián	annual; yearly
全集	quán jí	complete works; collected works	全球	quán qiú	the whole world
全景	quán jǐng	panorama; full view	全套	quán tào	complete set

Example:

我 们 全 家 人 出 去 了 。
Wǒ men quán jiā rén chū qu le
My family had gone out.

9

QUÁN   recover from illness

THE radical 疒 (originally 疒) represents a sick patient lying down (一) on a bed (爿). The phonetic 全 means finished or completed. The combination 痊 is based on the belief of physicians that when a disease (疒) has run its full course (全), the patient recovers: 痊.

丶 一 广 广 疒 疒 疒 疒 疒 疼 痊

痊愈   quán yù   fully recover from an illness

Example:

他 的 病 还 没 有 完 全 痊 愈 。
Tā de bìng hái méi yǒu wán quán quán yù
He has not fully recovered from his illness.

MǏ

rice
(uncooked)

米 is a pictograph of a rice stalk. Its original form depicted nine grains of rice ⁘ . This was modified to 米 and finally 米 , symbolising grains (Ⅹ) separated in the four quarters (十) by threshing. Although the rice-bowl may represent an honest means of living, "rice obtained by crookedness will not boil up into good food."

| 丶 | 丷 | 丷 | 半 | 米 | 米 | | | | | | | |

米波	mǐ bō	metric wave
米粉	mǐ fěn	rice-flour noodles; vermicelli
米酒	mǐ jiǔ	rice wine
米粒	mǐ lì	grain of rice
米色	mǐ sè	cream-coloured
米制	mǐ zhì	the metric system

Example:

这 米 煮 得 太 烂 了 。
Zhè mǐ zhǔ de tài làn le
This rice is overcooked.

11

粉

FĚN

powder

FACE powder in China was once made by grinding rice into fine particles. Hence the ideograph: 粉 meaning face powder — from 米 (rice) and 分 (divide, grind). The radical 米 is a likeness of a rice stalk and the phonetic 分 is a picture of a knife severing an object. 粉 now stands for anything ground into powder.

丶　丷　丷　半　半　米　米　粉　粉　粉

粉笔	fěn bǐ		chalk
粉刺	fěn cì		acne
粉红	fěn hóng		pink
粉身碎骨	fěn shēn suì gǔ		have one's body smashed to pieces; die the most cruel death
粉刷	fěn shuā		whitewash
粉丝	fěn sī		vermicelli made from bean starch, etc.
粉碎	fěn suì		smash; shatter; crush

Example:

他 把 米 磨 成 粉 。

Tā　bǎ　mǐ　mó　chéng　fěn

He grinds the rice into powder form.

精

JĪNG   refined; essence; vigour

米 (rice) is the radical of this character and 青 (green, pure) the phonetic. Rice, the only grain that grows in a padi field, is never mixed with other grains, and so signifies something pure. 青 (green) is also a symbol of purity; it is the colour of vegetation, 丹 representing the alchemist's stove and 生 the growing plant. The two symbols of purity combine to enforce the idea of refinement, essence or vigour: 米青.

丶 丷 ⺍ 扌 ⺶ 米 米一 米二 米扌 粠 粠 精 精 精

精兵	jīng bīng	picked troops; crack troops
精彩	jīng cǎi	brilliant; splendid; wonderful
精力	jīng lì	energy; vigour
精美	jīng měi	exquisite; elegant
精明强干	jīng míng qiáng gàn	capable; able and efficient
精疲力竭	jīng pí lì jié	exhausted; worn out

精巧	jīng qiǎo	exquisite; ingenious
精神	jīng shén	spirit; mind; vigour; drive
精心	jīng xīn	meticulously; elaborately
精液	jīng yè	seminal fluid; semen
精制	jīng zhì	made with extra care
精致	jīng zhì	fine; exquisite

Example:

这 花 瓶 的 雕 刻 很 精 致 。
Zhè huā píng de diāo kè hěn jīng zhì
The carvings on this vase are exquisite.

13

气(氣)

Qì breath; vapour; air

气 represents curling vapours rising and forming clouds. Ancient forms show the sun (☉) and fire (火) which cause the vapours: 炁. The regular form 氣, however, depicts the vapour (气) ascending from boiling rice (米) — now simplified to 气, meaning air, vapour, breath, energy or anger.

ノ 一 气 气 气

气冲冲	qì chōng chōng	furious; beside oneself with rage	
气喘	qì chuǎn	asthma	
气氛	qì fēn	atmosphere	
气愤	qì fèn	indignant; furious	

气候	qì hòu	climate
气力	qì lì	effort; energy; strength
气球	qì qiú	balloon
气温	qì wēn	air temperature
气象台	qì xiàng tái	meteorological observatory

Example:

会 谈 在 亲 切 友 好 的 气 氛 中 进 行 。
Huì tán zài qīng qiè yǒu hǎo de qì fēn zhōng jìn xíng

The talks were held in a cordial and friendly atmosphere.

14

SHÍ eat; food

食, to eat, is the radical relating to food in general. Its seal form shows that it is made up of 亼 (together) and 皀 (boiled grain, food). 皀 itself is a pictograph of the rice-pot (◇) and its contents (一) with a spoon or ladle (匕). 食 is the signal to come together (亼) to eat the food (皀). But food, like knowledge, needs to be properly digested. So: "Be quick over your work, but not over your food."

ノ 人 亽 今 今 食 食 食 食

月食	yuè shí	lunar eclipse
主食	zhǔ shí	staple food
食粮	shí liáng	grain; food
食品	shí pǐn	foodstuff; food; provisions
食谱	shí pǔ	recipes; cookbook

食宿	shí sù	board and lodging
食堂	shí táng	dining room; mess hall; canteen
食物	shí wù	food; eatables; edibles
食言	shí yán	go back on one's word; break one's promise
食指	shí zhǐ	index finger

Example:

米 是 亚 洲 人 的 主 食 。
Mǐ shì Yà zhōu rén de zhǔ shí

Rice is the staple food of Asians.

15

饭 (飯)

FÀN   rice (cooked)

飯, the character for cooked rice, comes from the radical 食 (food) and the phonetic 反 meaning return. 反 represents the repetitive motion (ナ) of the hand (又), as in eating (食). Although hungry people are not fastidious about food, "One speck of rat's dung spoils a whole pot of rice." In combination, 食 is simplified to 饣.

丿 勹 饣 饣 饣 饭 饭

饭菜	fàn cài	meal; repast
饭店	fàn diàn	restaurant
饭锅	fàn guō	pot for cooking rice; rice cooker
饭桶	fàn tǒng	rice bucket; big eater; good-for-nothing
饭碗	fàn wǎn	rice bowl; job; means of livelihood
饭桌	fàn zhuō	dining table

Example:

这 餐 厅 饭 菜 可 口 ， 服 务 又 周 到 。

Zhè cān tīng fàn cài kě kǒu   fú wù yòu zhōu dào

This restaurant offers tasty food and good service.

BǍO eat to the full

包 the phonetic combines with 食, the radical for food, to form 飽 (satiated). The seal form of 包 is 🄑, depicting a foetus enclosed in the body; hence the meaning wrapped up. 飽 therefore means food all wrapped up in the stomach, i.e., fully satisfied. However, as the saying goes: "Better be hungry and pure than well-filled and corrupt."

ノ	ク	ゟ	ゟ	饣	饣	饣	饱						

饱含	bǎo hán	filled with
饱和	bǎo hé	saturation
饱满	bǎo mǎn	full; plump
饱学	bǎo xué	learned

Example:

她 的 眼 睛 饱 含 着 幸 福 的 热 泪 。
Tā de yǎn jīng bǎo hán zhe xìng fú de rè lèi

Her eyes were filled with tears of joy.

17

饿(餓)

È hungry

THIS character is based on the radical for food: 食. It literally means feed (食) me (我) — a fitting sign for hunger. Another character for hunger is 饑, literally: little (幾) food (食), simplified to 饥, i.e., food (饣) on small table (几). Although hunger is no respecter of persons, "**Even** a hungry person will refuse food offered in contempt."

ノ	ク	乞	饣	饣	钟	饣	饿	饿	饿				

挨饿	āi è	go hungry
饥饿	jī è	hunger; starvation
饿虎扑食	è hǔ pū shí	like a hungry tiger pouncing on its prey

Example:

他 挣 扎 在 饥 饿 线 上 。
Tā zhēng zhá zài jī è xiàn shang

She struggled along on the verge of death.

館(館)

THE food radical 食 combines with 官 to produce 館, a public building. The phonetic 官 (official) originally meant the residence of an official — the hall (宀) of the city (🄰). 食 (food) together with 官 suggests a public building doing food business — inn, hotel or restaurant. Hence: "An innkeeper never worries if your appetite is big."

GUǍN hotel; restaurant

| 丿 | 𠂊 | 饣 | 饣 | 饣 | 馆 | 馆 | 馆 | 馆 | 馆 | 馆 | | | |

旅馆	lǚ guǎn	hotel
美术馆	měi shù guǎn	art gallery
体育馆	tǐ yù guǎn	gymnasium; stadium
图书馆	tú shū guǎn	library

Example:

这 旅 馆 的 布 置 很 堂 皇 。
Zhè lǚ guǎn de bù zhì hěn táng huáng
The hotel's decor is very impressive.

饮(飲)

YǏN   drink

BASED on the food radical 食, this character has a significant phonetic 欠, suggesting breath. 欠 originally was a pictograph of a man opening his mouth to catch his breath, as in drinking: 欠. This was modified to 旡, representing air waves (彡) emanating from the man (儿). The primitive form of the character for drink shows clearly a drinking flask (酉) as part of the food radical.

丿 ㇀ 饣 饮 饮 饮 饮

饮茶	yǐn chá	drink tea
饮弹	yǐn dàn	be hit by a bullet
饮恨	yǐn hèn	nurse a grievance
饮料	yǐn liào	drink; beverage
饮泣	yǐn qì	weep in silence
饮食	yǐn shí	food and drink; diet
饮用水	yǐn yòng shuǐ	drinking water; potable water

Example:

他 喜 欢 早 上 在 茶 楼 饮 茶 。

Tā   xǐ   huān   zǎo   shang   zài   chá   lóu   yǐn   chá

He likes to drink tea at the teahouse in the morning.

车 (車)

CHĒ
cart;
carriage;
chariot

車 represents a bird's eye view of a cart, showing its body (曰), the two wheels (二) and the axle (|). The primitive forms of 車 are as varied as carts, carriages and chariots. But, whatever the form, where there is a cart in front there is a track behind; so "Take warning from the wrecked cart ahead of you."

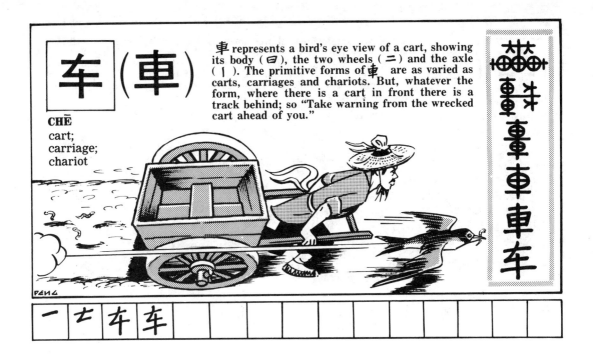

一 ナ 车 车

汽车	qì chē	motor vehicle; automobile	
车床	chē chuáng	lathe	
车费	chē fèi	fare	
车祸	chē huò	road accident	
车间	chē jiān	workshop	
车辆	chē liàng	vehicle; car	
车轮	chē lún	wheel (of a vehicle)	
车票	chē piào	train or bus ticket	
车水马龙	chē shuǐ mǎ lóng	heavy traffic	
车速	chē sù	speed of a motor vehicle	
车胎	chē tāi	tyre	
车站	chē zhàn	station; depot; stop	

Example:

这 条 街 的 汽 车 真 多 。
Zhè tiáo jiē de qì chē zhēn duō

This street is full of vehicles.

21

轰（轟）is the triple form of the noisy cart (車). It serves as a fitting symbol for any loud or explosive sound like the rumbling of many carts. In the simplified form, 又 (again; ditto) replaces each of the two lower carts to produce 轰. 又 itself is a simplified picture of the right hand; and the right hand, returning repeatedly to the mouth in eating, suggests "again".

HŌNG   bang; boom (noise; uproar)

| 一 | 土 | 车 | 车 | 轰 | 轰 | 轰 | 轰 | | | | |

轰动	hōng dòng	cause a sensation; make a stir
轰轰烈烈	hōng hōng liè liè	on a grand and spectacular scale; vigorous; dynamic
轰击	hōng jī	shell; bombard
轰隆	hōng lōng	rumble; roll
轰鸣	hōng míng	thunder; roar
轰炸	hōng zhà	bomb

Example:

她 的 超 级 迷 你 裙 使 全 场 轰 动 起 来 。
Tā de chāo jí mí nǐ qún shǐ quán chǎng hōng dòng qǐ lái
Her ultra-miniskirt caused a stir at the party.

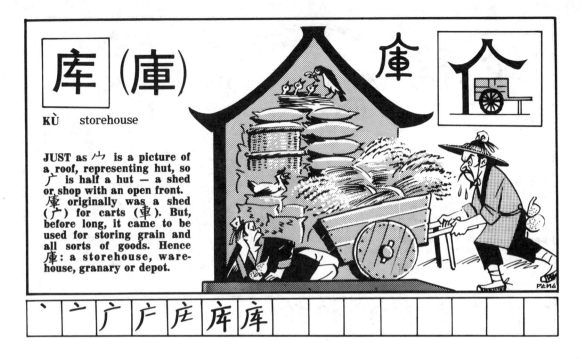

库(庫)

KÙ   storehouse

JUST as 宀 is a picture of a roof, representing hut, so 广 is half a hut — a shed or shop with an open front. 庫 originally was a shed (广) for carts (車). But, before long, it came to be used for storing grain and all sorts of goods. Hence 庫: a storehouse, warehouse, granary or depot.

`、　宀　广　广　庄　库　库`

军械库	jūn xiè kù	armoury
仓库	cāng kù	storehouse; warehouse
库藏	kù cáng	have in storage
库存	kù cún	stock; reserve
库房	kù fáng	storehouse

Example:

这 仓 库 可 以 容 纳 大 量 货 物 。
Zhè cāng kù kě yǐ róng nà dà liàng huò wù
This warehouse can accomodate a large amount of goods.

23

轮 (輪)

LÚN

wheel

輪, the wheel that moves the cart, has 車 (cart) for radical. 侖, its phonetic, is suggestive, not only of the orderly arrangement of the spokes of a wheel, but also their unity and stability. It signifies a collection (亼) of ancient documents preserved on bamboo slips tied together in an orderly manner (冊).

一	七	车	车	车'	车∧	轮	轮				

轮班	lún bān	in shifts; in relays	轮廓	lún kuò	outline; contour; rough sketch
轮齿	lún chǐ	teeth of a cogwheel	轮流	lún liú	take turns; do something in turn
轮船	lún chuán	steamer	轮胎	lún tāi	tyre
轮渡	lún dù	ferry	轮椅	lún yǐ	wheelchair
轮换	lún huàn	rotate; take turns	轮轴	lún zhóu	wheel and axle
轮机	lún jī	turbine	轮子	lún zi	wheel

Example:

这 个 车 轮 被 刮 坏 了 。

Zhè ge chē lún bèi guā huài le

The wheel of this car was badly scratched.

24

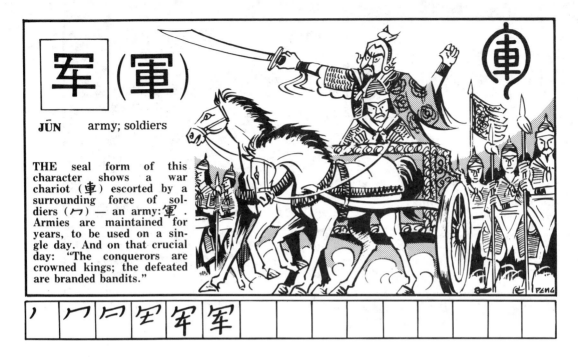

军 (軍)

JŪN   army; soldiers

THE seal form of this character shows a war chariot (車) escorted by a surrounding force of soldiers (勹) — an army: 軍. Armies are maintained for years, to be used on a single day. And on that crucial day: "The conquerors are crowned kings; the defeated are branded bandits."

丿	冖	冖	冟	军	军						

军备	jūn bèi	armament; arms	
军部	jūn bù	army headquarters	
军操	jūn cāo	military drill	
军车	jūn chē	military vehicle	
军队	jūn duì	armed forces	
军法	jūn fǎ	military criminal code	
军港	jūn gǎng	naval port	
军官	jūn guān	officer	

军火	jūn huǒ	arms and ammunition	
军力	jūn lì	military strength	
军人	jūn rén	soldier; serviceman	
军士	jūn shì	noncommissioned officer (NCO)	
军事训练	jūn shì xùn liàn	military training	
军事演习	jūn shì yǎn xí	military manoeuvre; war exercise	
军营	jūn yíng	military camp; barracks	

Example:

军 人 的 工 作 是 很 有 挑 战 性 的 。
Jūn rén de gōng zuò shi hěn yǒu tiǎo zhàn xìng de
The work of a soldier is full of challenges.

斩 (斬)

ZHǍN　　chop off

斩 probably has reference to a war chariot (車) with warriors wielding axes (斤) to cut off the enemy. It may also mean to whirl or brandish (車) a battle axe (斤). But cutting off an enemy does not eradicate the source of trouble; hence the saying: "When cutting the weeds, get rid of the root" (斩草除根).

| 一 | 土 | 车 | 车 | 车' | 斩 | 斩 | 斩 | | | | | |

斩草除根	zhǎn cǎo chú gēn	destroy root and branch — stamp out the source of trouble
斩钉截铁	zhǎn dīng jié tiě	resolute and decisive; categorical
斩断	zhǎn duàn	chop off
斩首	zhàn shǒu	behead; decapitate

Example:

他 的 手 被 机 器 斩 断 了 。
Tā de shǒu bèi jī qì zhǎn duàn le

His hands were chopped off by the machine.

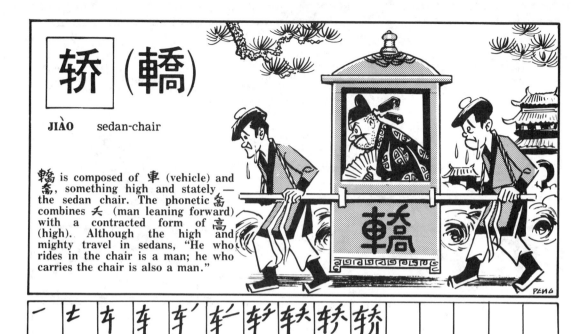

轿 (轎)

JIÀO   sedan-chair

轎 is composed of 車 (vehicle) and 喬, something high and stately — the sedan chair. The phonetic 喬 combines 夭 (man leaning forward) with a contracted form of 高 (high). Although the high and mighty travel in sedans, "He who rides in the chair is a man; he who carries the chair is also a man."

一 士 车 车 车′ 轩 轩 轩 轿 轿

轿车	jiào chē	car
轿子	jiào zi	sedan chair
花轿	huā jiào	bridal sedan chair

Example:

古 时 候 的 华 人 新 娘 是 坐 花 轿 的 。

Gǔ shí huò de huá rén xīn niáng shi zuò huā jiào de

In the olden days, Chinese brides rode on bridal sedan chairs.

软 (軟)

RUǍN

soft; weak;
pliable
yielding;

THE mobility of the carriage (車) is used to good effect in this character. Combined with 欠, it produces 軟, meaning soft and weak or pliable and flexible, 欠 signifying a man (儿) gasping for breath (彡), i.e., exhausted, deficient. 軟 may also be written 輭, the phonetic 耎 representing the soft beard (而) of a man (大).

一 十 车 车 车 轫 软 软

软钢	ruǎn gāng	mild steel; soft steel
软骨头	ruǎn gú tou	a weak-kneed person; a spineless person; a coward
软骨	ruǎn gǔ	cartilage
软化	ruǎn huà	soften; win over by soft tactics
软和	ruǎn huo	gentle; kind; soft
软件	ruǎn jiàn	software
软禁	ruǎn jìn	put somebody under house arrest
软弱	ruǎn ruò	weak; feeble; flabby

Example:

她 被 他 的 甜 言 蜜 语 软 化 了 。
Tā bèi tā de tián yán mì yǔ ruǎn huà le
She was won over by his sweet words.

28

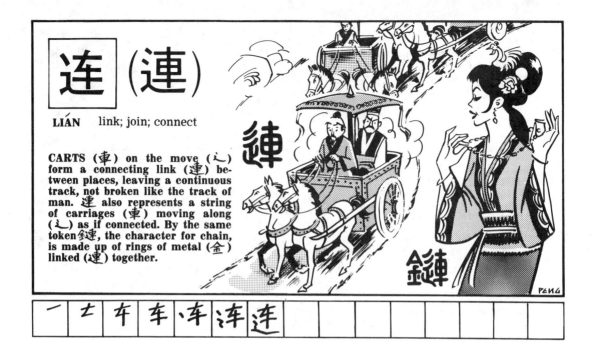

连 (連)

LIÁN link; join; connect

CARTS (車) on the move (辶) form a connecting link (連) between places, leaving a continuous track, not broken like the track of man. 連 also represents a string of carriages (車) moving along (辶) as if connected. By the same token 鏈, the character for chain, is made up of rings of metal (金) linked (連) together.

一 士 车 车 车 连 连

连贯	lián guàn	link up; piece together; hang together; coherent; consistent
连环画	lián huán huà	a book (usually for children) with a story told in pictures; picture story book
连累	lián lěi	implicate; involve; get somebody into trouble
连忙	lián máng	promptly; at once
连日	lián rì	for days on end; day after day
连同	lián tóng	together with; along with
连续	lián xù	continuous; successive
连夜	lián yè	the same night; that very night

Example:

小 梅 喜 欢 看 香 港 的 连 续 剧 。
Xiǎo méi xǐ huān kàn Xiāng Gǎng de lián xù jù
Xiaomei likes to watch the Hongkong serialised dramas.

29

莲 (蓮)

LIÁN lotus

蓮 the lotus, is a prolific water plant (艹) that spreads continuously (連) like a flowery chain. It epitomises purity because it grows out of mud but remains undefiled. From 連 (connect) also comes the character 漣 (ripples) based on the water radical 氵 — ripples being a continuous succession (連) of waves.

一 十 艹 艼 芒 苹 莒 萍 莲 莲

莲花	lián huā	lotus flower
莲蓬	lián peng	seedpod of the lotus
莲蓬头	lián peng tóu	shower nozzle
莲子	lián zǐ	lotus seed

Example:

莲 花 是 生 长 在 水 里 的 。
Lián huā shì shēng zhǎng zài shuǐ lǐ de
Lotus flowers grow in water.

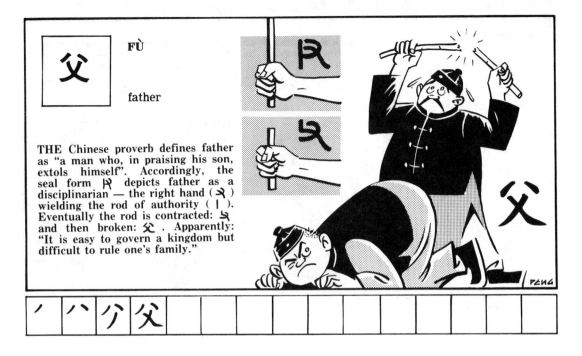

父 FÙ

father

THE Chinese proverb defines father as "a man who, in praising his son, extols himself". Accordingly, the seal form 𝖋 depicts father as a disciplinarian — the right hand (又) wielding the rod of authority (｜). Eventually the rod is contracted: 𝖋 and then broken: 父 . Apparently: "It is easy to govern a kingdom but difficult to rule one's family."

ノ 八 分 父

父母	fù mǔ	father and mother; parents
父亲	fù qin	father
父权制	fù quán zhì	patriarchy
父兄	fù xiōng	father and elder brothers; head of a family

Example:

我 的 父 亲 是 个 慈 祥 的 人 。
Wǒ de fù qin shì ge cí xiáng de rén
My father is a kindly person.

31

JĪN

巾

napkin; towel;
handkerchief

巾 is a pictograph of a small piece of cloth used for cleaning, dusting or wiping. In ancient times it was worn, suspended from the girdle. 冂 represents the two extremities of the cloth hanging (|) from the girdle. 巾 forms the radical of a series of characters relating to cloth in general.

| 丨 | 冂 | 巾 | | | | | | | | | | | |

巾帼	jīn guó	woman
巾帼英雄	jīn guó yīng xióng	a heroine
餐巾	cān jīn	napkin
手巾	shǒu jīn	hand towel
头巾	tóu jīn	headdress
围巾	wéi jīn	scarf

Example:

她 用 手 巾 抹 脸 。

Tā yòng shǒu jīn ma liǎn

She uses the towel to wipe her face.

BÙ

cloth

THIS character is based on the radical for cloth: 巾 . The phonetic 父 (father) is discernible as 又 in the seal form 旁 . 又 is a picture of the right hand (又) with the rod of authority (|), and implies discipline, control and order — as essential in weaving as in marrying. So the saying goes: "Hasty weaving produces shoddy cloth; a girl who marries in haste has a fool for a husband."

一 ナ ナ 右 布

布道	bù dào	preach
布丁	bù dīng	pudding
布防	bù fáng	place troops on garrison duty
布告	bù gào	notice; bulletin; proclamation
布谷鸟	bù gǔ niǎo	cuckoo
布匹	bù pǐ	cloth; piece goods
布置	bù zhì	fix up; arrange; decorate; assign; make arrangements for; give instructions about

Example:

用 这 匹 布 做 成 衣 服 ， 一 定 很 漂 亮 。

Yòng zhè pǐ bù zuò chéng yī fu   yī dìng hěn piào liàng

This cloth will make a pretty dress.

33

ZHŎU

broom;
duster

IN the seal form 帚, broom is suggested by a hand (彐) with an improvised broom (帚) — double cloth (巾) attached to a handle (丨). Although a helping hand (扌) can easily turn 帚 (broom) into 掃 (sweep), "no one will sweep a public hall used by everyone."

| フ | ㇆ | ヨ | ㇕ | 彐 | 帚 | 帚 | 帚 | | | | | | |

| 扫帚 | sào zhǒu | broom |
| 扫帚星 | sào zhǒu xīng | comet |

Example:

妈 妈 最 近 买 了 一 把 新 扫 帚 。

Mā ma zuì jìn mǎi le yì bǎ xīn sào zhǒu

Mother bought a new broom recently.

34

妇 (婦)

FÙ   wife; married woman

WOMAN (女) with broom (帚) is the symbol for wife or married woman: 婦, simplified to 妇 — woman (女) with helping hand (彐). Another character for wife is 妻 — woman (女) with broom (十) in hand (彐). Whatever the character, "She who is the wife of one man cannot eat the rice of two."

〈	女	女	妇	妇	妇							

少妇	shào fù	young married woman
夫妇	fū fù	husband and wife
妇产科	fù chǎn kē	(department of) gynaecology and obstetrics
妇女	fù nǚ	woman
妇人	fù rén	married woman
妇幼	fù yòu	women and children

Example:

这 位 少 妇 真 勇 敢 ， 为 了 丈 夫 不 惜 牺 牲 一 切 。
Zhè wèi shào fù zhēn yǒng gǎn   wèi le zhàng fū bù xì xī shēng yí qiè
She's a brave young woman. She sacrificed herself for the sake of her husband.

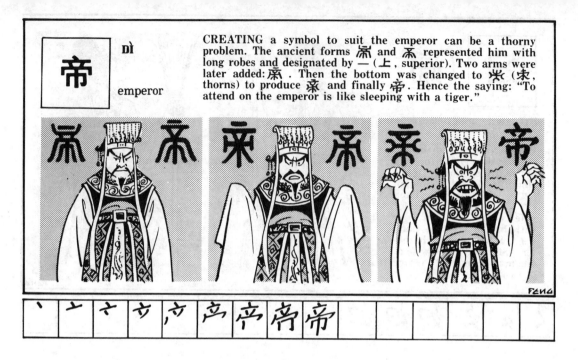

帝 DÌ emperor

CREATING a symbol to suit the emperor can be a thorny problem. The ancient forms 帝 and 帝 represented him with long robes and designated by 一 (上, superior). Two arms were later added: 帝. Then the bottom was changed to 朿 (朿, thorns) to produce 帝 and finally 帝. Hence the saying: "To attend on the emperor is like sleeping with a tiger."

皇帝	huáng dì	emperor
上帝	shàng dì	God
帝国	dì guó	empire
帝国主义	dì guó zhǔ yì	imperialism
帝王	dì wáng	emperor; monarch
帝制	dì zhì	autocratic monarchy; monarchy

Example:

秦 始 皇 是 中 国 第 一 个 皇 帝 。
Qín shǐ huáng shì Zhōng Guó dì yī ge huáng dì
Qinshihuang was the first emperor of China.

DÀI   girdle; bring

帯 is a pictograph of the ancient girdle, embellished with trinkets hanging from it: 卅. At the bottom of the character are the robes, represented by 帀 — two 巾, one over the other. 带 also means to bring or take along, as articles are often carried, tucked in or worn at the girdle.

一 十 卅 卅 卅 芇 芇 带 带

录音带	lù yīn dài	recording tape
热带	rè dài	the tropics
带累	dài lěi	implicate; involve
带领	dài lǐng	lead; guide
带路	dài lù	show the way; act as a guide
带头	dài tóu	take the lead; be the first

Example:

老 师 带 领 一 群 学 生 去 爬 山 。
Lǎo shī dài lǐng yī qún xué shēng qù pá shān

The teacher led a group of students for a climb in the mountain.

37

帽

MÀO

hat;
cap

THE phonetic 冒 means rash, acting with eyes (目) covered (冃).
冃 indicates a cover (冂) for something (一), viz., the head (一).
冒 combines with the radical 巾 (cloth) to produce 帽 (hat, cap). A
cap does not always fit the head of the wearer because "many a good
man can be found under a shabby hat."

| 丨 | 冂 | 巾 | 巾' | 巾冂 | 巾冃 | 帽 | 巾冒 | 帽 | 帽 | 帽 | 帽 |

安全帽　　ān chuán mào　　safety helmet

帽徽　　　mào huī　　　insignia on a cap

帽子　　　mào zi　　　headgear; hat; cap; label; tag; brand

Example:

当 上 工 地 时 ， 请 记 得 带 上 安 全 帽 。

Dāng shàng gōng dì shí　qing jì dé dài shàng ān quán mào

Please remember to put on the safety helmet when you are at the work site.

38

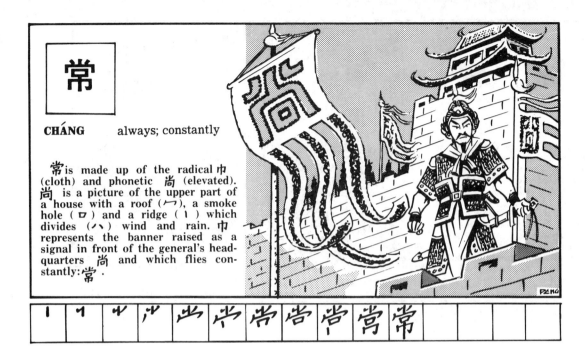

常

CHÁNG   always; constantly

常 is made up of the radical 巾 (cloth) and phonetic 尚 (elevated). 尚 is a picture of the upper part of a house with a roof (宀), a smoke hole (口) and a ridge (丨) which divides (八) wind and rain. 巾 represents the banner raised as a signal in front of the general's headquarters 尚 and which flies constantly: 常.

丨 丩 丩 丷 屵 屵 屵 岩 常 常 常

常备军	cháng bèi jūn	standing army
常常	cháng cháng	frequently; generally
常会	cháng huì	regular meeting
常见	cháng jiàn	common
常年	cháng nián	throughout the year; perennial
常人	cháng rén	man in the street

常识	cháng shí	general or elementary knowledge
常态	cháng tài	normal behaviour or conditions
常务	cháng wù	day-to-day business; routine
常言道	cháng yán dào	as the saying goes
常用	cháng yòng	in common use
常驻	cháng zhù	resident; permanent

Example:

她 常 常 去 听 音 乐 会 。

Tā cháng cháng qu tīng yīn yuè huà

She goes to the concerts very often.

帮 (幫)

BĀNG　　help; assist

IN feudal times the emperor relied on the support of his nobles. The seal form of the character for such aid combines 봙 with 帛. 봙 denotes the crops (坐) and land (土) under the noble's rule (彐). 帛 signifies the silk or wealth donated.

In the modern form the phonetic 邦 means state or country represented by woods (丰) and city (阝).

一　二　三　丰　邦　邦　邦　帮　帮

帮忙	bāng máng	help; give a hand; do a favour
帮手	bāng shou	helper; assistant
帮凶	bāng xiōng	accomplice; accessary
帮助	bāng zhù	help; assist

Example:

我　想　把　这　箱　水　果　搬　到　那　里　，　你　能　帮　我　吗　？
Wǒ xiǎng bǎ zhè xiāng shuǐ guǒ bān dào nà lǐ　　nǐ néng bāng wǒ ma

Can you help me to carry the carton of fruits there?

40

衣

yī clothes

衣 delineates the outlines of clothing: on the top, the outer garments with sleeves; at the bottom, the flowing robes. This pictograph serves as a radical for characters relating to clothing. Apparently, clothes do not make the man, according to the saying: "You can change the clothes; you cannot change the man."

PENG

丶	亠	产	产	衣	衣								

衣橱	yī chú	wardrobe
衣服	yī fu	clothing; clothes
衣冠楚楚	yī guān chǔ chǔ	be immaculately dressed
衣冠禽兽	yī guān qín shòu	a beast in human attire; brute
衣架	yī jià	coat hanger; clothes-rack
衣食住行	yī shí zhù xíng	food, clothing, shelter and transportation – basic necessities of life
衣鱼	yī yú	silverfish; fish moth; bookworm

Example:

这 件 衣 服 是 新 买 的 ！
Zhè jiàn yī fu shì xīn mǎi de

This dress is newly bought!

41

裤 (褲)

KÙ trousers

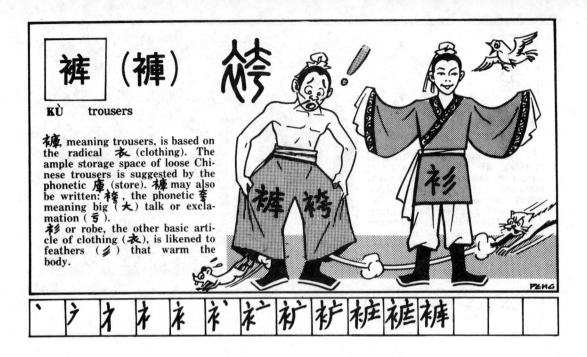

褲 meaning trousers, is based on the radical 衣 (clothing). The ample storage space of loose Chinese trousers is suggested by the phonetic 庫 (store). 裤 may also be written: 誇, the phonetic 夸 meaning big (大) talk or exclamation (亏).

衫 or robe, the other basic article of clothing (衣), is likened to feathers (彡) that warm the body.

丶 亠 才 礻 礻 礻 衤 衤 衤 衤 裤 裤

| 短裤 | duǎn kù | shorts |
| 裤子 | kù zi | trousers; pants |

Example:

这 条 裤 子 太 短 了 ， 不 能 穿 。
Zhè tiáo kù zi tài duǎn le bù néng chuāng

This pair of pants is too short.

被 **BÈI**

bedclothes; blankets

被, bedclothes or blankets, are regarded as cloth (衣) skin (皮). The phonetic 皮 or 爰, represents the skin (彡) flayed by hand (彐) with knife (丿). 被 may also mean to suffer, a sign of the passive. However, 袍 (literally, cloth 衣 wrap 包) refers to the long robe or outer garment wrapped round the body to keep it warm and active.

丶 冫 衤 衤 衤 衤 衭 衭 衭 衭 被 被

被捕	bèi bǔ	be arrested; be under arrest
被单	bèi dān	(bed) sheet
被动	bèi dòng	passive
被俘	bèi fú	be captured; be taken prisoner
被告	bèi gào	defendant; the accused
被害人	bèi hài rén	the injured party; the victim
被迫	bèi pò	be compelled; be forced; be constrained
被褥	bèi rù	bedding; bedclothes

Example:

天 气 好 冷 ， 记 得 盖 被 。

Tiān qì hǎo lěng　　jì de gài bèi

It's cold. Remember to pull up your blanket.

43

表

BIǍO

express;
show;
manifest

表 combining 衣 with 毛, means to show or make known. Clothes (衣) were originally skins with hair (毛) on the outside. 表 literally means the outside of clothes — the manifestation or outer appearance which may be a false front. It is said that when a boy is small you can see the man, but "A man cannot be known by his looks, nor can the sea be measured with a bushel basket."

一 二 士 圭 圭 圭 表 表

表层	biǎo céng	surface layer
表达	biǎo dá	express; convey; voice
表格	biǎo gé	form; table
表决	biǎo jué	decide by vote; vote
表露	biǎo lù	show; reveal
表面	biǎo miàn	surface; face; outside; appearance
表明	biǎo míng	make known; make clear
表亲	biǎo qīn	cousin; cousinship
表情	biǎo qíng	express one's feelings; expression
表示	biǎo shì	show; express; indicate
表现	biǎo xiàn	manifestation; display; manifest

Example:

对 这 问 题 他 没 有 表 明 立 场 。

Duì zhè wèn tí tā méi yǒu biǎo míng lì chǎng

He did not express his stand on this matter.

片

Man cannot wait to saw a tree (木) vertically into two halves: 爿 and 片. 爿 serves as a strong plank for his bed and 片 as a symbol for a slice or piece. With 爿 and 片 he forms a tripod for an urn: 鼎. He uses 木 and its components 爿 and 片 as radicals. And so the saying goes: "He plants a tree in the morning and wants to saw planks from it in the evening."

PIÀN   slice; piece

| ノ | 丿 | 爿 | 片 | | | | | | | | | | |

片段	piàn duàn	part; passage; extract; fragment
片刻	piàn kè	a short while; an instant; a moment
片时	piàn shí	a short while; a moment
片瓦无存	piàn wǎ wú cún	not a single tile remains — be razed to the ground
片言	piàn yán	a few words; a phrase or two
片子	piàn zi	flat, thin piece; slice; flake; scrap

Example:

他 在 这 里 逗 留 了 片 刻 。
Tā zài zhè lǐ dòu líu le piàn kè
He was here for a short while.

45

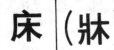

床 (牀)

CHUÁNG bed

爿, the left half of a tree (木), represents a thick, strong plank used for a bed. By adding 爿 to 木 you can make 牀 (bed) — literally, strong plank (爿) of wood (木). Another way is by placing 木 (wood) under 广 (roof): 床. As you make your bed, you must lie on it, so "if you can't sleep, don't complain about your bed."

丶　亠　广　广　庁　庄　床

单人床	dān rén chuáng	single bed
双人床	shuāng rén chuáng	double bed
床单	chuáng dān	bedsheet
床垫	chuáng diàn	mattress
床位	chuáng wèi	berth; bunk; bed
床罩	chuáng zhào	bedspread

Example:

他 卧 病 在 床 。

Tā　wò　bìng　zài　chuáng

He is sick in bed.

墙（牆）

QIÁNG wall

THE seal form of the phonetic 嗇 signifies grain (來) stored within (入) a double-walled granary (回). The idea of wall is reinforced by the radical 爿, a symbol of strength. Since walls are made of clay or earth (土), the character may also be written: 墻. Walls may fortify a city, but "men, not walls, make a city."

一 十 土 圹 圹 圹 坮 垆 坪 墶 墙 墙 墙

墙壁	qiáng bì	wall
墙角	qiáng jiǎo	a corner formed by two walls
墙脚	qiáng jiǎo	the foot of a wall; foundation

Example·

墙 壁 上 有 一 个 大 洞 。

Qiáng bì shang yǒu yī ge dà dòng

There is a big hole on the wall.

将 (將)

将 has many seal forms and varied meanings:

is a meatblock (月) with meat (肉).

shows the meatblock (月) with meat (夕) and salt (卤).

represents the meatblock (月) with meat (夕) and brine (卤).

signifies the hand (彐) placing meat (夕) upon the block (月).

JIĀNG take; hold; handle; shall; will

Hence the extended meanings: offer, present; nourish, help; take, hold; handle, manage. 将 is a character with a future, often used for shall or will; it is even used to mean leader or general.

PENG

`	冫	爿	爿	爿	爿	爿	将	将					

将错就错	jiāng cuò jiù cuò	leave a mistake uncorrected and make the best of it
将计就计	jiāng jì jiù jì	turn somebody's trick against him; beat somebody at his own game
将近	jiāng jìn	close to; nearly; almost
将军	jiāng jūn	general
将来	jiāng lái	future

Example:

我 将 请 他 来 我 家 。

Wǒ jiāng qǐng tā lái wǒ jiā

I am inviting him over to my house.

壮 (壯)

ZHUÀNG

strong;
eminent;
impressive

壯士 literally means a strong and impressive (爿) person-age (士) or one who professes to be so; by extension, strong and able-bodied.

An analogous character is 妝 (adorn, disguise) — an impressive (爿) woman (女), i.e., one who adorns herself with make-up.

| 、 | 丶 | 爿 | 爿- | -爿+ | 壮 | | | | | | | | |

壮胆	zhuàng dǎn	embolden; boost somebody's courage
壮丽	zhuàng lì	majestic; magnificent; glorious
壮烈	zhuàng liè	heroic; brave
壮士	zhuàng shì	hero; warrior
壮实	zhuàng shi	sturdy; robust
壮志	zhuàng zhì	great aspiration; lofty ideal

Example:

他 为 国 壮 烈 牺 牲 。

Tā wèi guó zhuàng liè xī shēng

He sacrificed heroically for his country.

49

装 （裝）

ZHUĀNG　pack; fill; pretend

壯, the phonetic, means strong or robust. It was originally applied to an official distinguished by his robe of office, and therefore has to do with appearance. The addition of the radical 衣 (clothing) suggests putting oneself into another's clothing and filling it — to deceive; by extension, to pack, fill, pretend: 裝.

丶 丷 ＞ 丬 爿 壯 壯 壯 裝 裝 裝 裝

装扮	zhuāng bàn	dress up; disguise
装备	zhuāng bèi	equip; equipment; outfit
装糊涂	zhuāng hú tu	pretend not to know
装货	zhuāng huò	loading (cargo)
装甲车	zhuāng jiǎ chē	armoured car
装模作样	zhuāng mú zuò yàng	be affected; put on an act
装配	zhuāng pèi	assemble; fit together

装腔	zhuāng qiāng	behave affectedly; be artificial
装饰	zhuāng shì	decorate; adorn; ornament; deck
装束	zhuāng shù	dress; attire
装修	zhuāng xiū	fit up (a house, etc.)
装置	zhuāng zhì	install; fit; installation

Example:

她 装 老 大 娘 真 象 。
Tā zhuāng Lǎo dà niáng zhēn xiàng
She acted like an old lady.

夕

xī

evening

夕 is a picture of the crescent moon emerging on the horizon at dusk, its lower part obstructed by a mountain. Hence the extended meaning: dusk, evening. To man, the rising moon presents opportunities but the proverb laments: "How seldom in life is the moon directly overhead!"

| ノ | ク | 夕 | | | | | | | | | | |

一朝一夕	yī zhāo yī xī	overnight
夕烟	xī yān	evening mist
夕阳	xī yáng	the setting sun
夕照	xī zhào	the glow of the setting sun; evening glow

Example:

这 些 问 题 不 是 一 朝 一 夕 能 够 解 决 的 。

Zhè xie wèn tí bú shì yī zhāo yī xī néng gòu jiě jué de

These problems cannot be solved overnight.

DUŌ

多

many;
much

From morning to evening man toiled in the field, and evening (夕) after evening (夕) he noted the fruitage of his labour. "Many evenings" (多) soon came to mean "many". His hard work bore much (多) fruit (果), producing a new word: 夥 (fruitful) and demonstrating the principle: "Sow much, reap much; sow little, reap little."

ノ	ク	夕	多	多	多						

多半	duō bàn	the greater part; most
多才多艺	duō cái duō yì	versatile; gifted in many ways
多此一举	duō cǐ yì jǔ	make an unnecessary move
多方面	duō fāng miàn	many-sided; in many ways
多国公司	duō guó gōng sī	multinational corporation
多民族	duō mín zú	
国家	guó jiā	multinational country

多少	duō shǎo	amount; somewhat; how many
多时	duō shí	a long time
多谢	duō xiè	thanks a lot
多心	duō xīn	oversensitive; suspicious
多余	duō yú	unnecessary; superfluous
多嘴	duō zuǐ	speak out of turn

Example:

你 的 担 心 是 多 余 的 。
Nǐ de dān xīn shì duō yú de
Your worries are unnecessary.

夠

GÒU

enough

句 is to hook (勹) with the mouth (口): to entice; 多 means much, many. 夠 therefore signifies to entice many, i.e., enough. But enough is not always enough, according to the proverb: "To complete a thing, a hundred years is not sufficient; to destroy it, a day is more than enough."

丿 勹 夕 夕 多 多 多 夠 夠 夠 夠

够本	gòu běn	break even
够朋友	gòu péng you	be a friend indeed
够受的	gòu shòu de	quite an ordeal
够意思	gòu yì si	really something; terrific; generous; really kind

Example:

这 场 球 赛 可 真 够 意 思 。
Zhè cháng qiú sài kě zhēn gòu yì si

That was really a terrific game.

DIĒ

father;
daddy

It takes three desperate characters to represent father:
父 is raised hand (又) wielding a rod (l).
爹 incorporates 多 — much raising of hand with rod.
爸 includes 巴 — poised like a snake, ready to strike.
All of them exemplify the saying, "It is easier to rule a nation than a son."

爸爸	bà ba	papa; dad; father
爹爹	diē die	father; dad; papa
爹娘	diē niáng	parents
父老	fù lǎo	elders (of a country or district)
父母	fù mǔ	father and mother; parents
父亲	fù qīn	father
父系亲属	fù xì qīn shǔ	relatives on the paternal side

Example:

父 亲 节 那 天 ， 我 送 爸 爸 一 份 礼 物 。
Fù qīn jié nà tiān wǒ sòng bà ba yí fèn lǐ wù
On Father's Day, I gave my father a present.

54

外

WÀI
outside

外 is composed of 夕 (evening) and 卜 (divine). Divination (卜), by interpreting the vertical (|) and horizontal (-) cracks of a heated tortoise-shell, was deemed effective only before (or outside of) evening. Hence the meaning: outside or foreign. And for such outside or foreign help, many will pay handsomely — those who place trust in the saying: "Much money moves the gods."

丿 夕 夕 列 外

外币	wài bì	foreign currency
外边	wài bian	outside; out
外表	wài biǎo	outward appearance; exterior
外宾	wài bīn	foreign guest
外公	wài gōng	(maternal) grandfather
外国	wài guó	foreign country
外行	wài háng	layman; nonprofessional
外籍	wài jí	foreign nationality
外交	wài jiāo	diplomacy; foreign affairs
外快	wài kuài	extra income
外贸	wài mào	foreign trade
外貌	wài mào	appearance; looks
外人	wài rén	stranger; outsider
外孙	wài sūn	daughter's son; grandson
外套	wài tào	overcoat

Example:

我 对 音 乐 很 外 行 。

Wǒ duì yīn yùe hěn wài háng

I am a layman in music.

梦 (夢)

MÈNG　dream

The seal forms of dream are horrifying enough to evoke a nightmare. No wonder the original character; 瞢 means bad sight (苜) with covered (冖) eyes (目). Dreams being evening visions, 夕 replaces 目 in the new form: 夢 , now simplified to 梦 (evening trees) — a pleasant dream. Unfortunately, "a beautiful dream is soon ended."

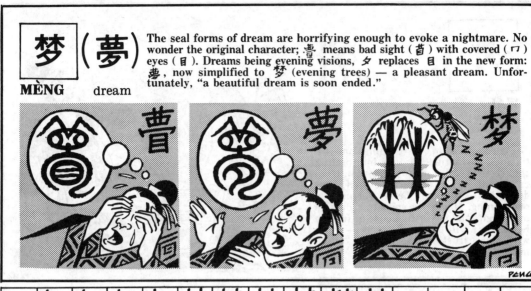

梦话	mèng huà	words uttered in one's sleep; somniloquy
梦幻	mèng huàn	illusion; dream; reverie
梦境	mèng jìng	dreamland; dreamworld; dream
梦想	mèng xiǎng	dream of; vainly hope
梦游症	mèng yóu zhèng	somnambulism; sleepwalking

Example:

昨 晚 我 听 见 你 说 梦 话 。

Zuó wǎn wǒ tīng jiàn nǐ shuō mèng huà

I heard you talk in your sleep last night.

夜 YÈ night

The seal character 夜 depicts man (大) sleeping on his side (ノ) in the evening (夕). The modern form 夜 shows man (亻) under cover (亠) lying on his other side (㇏) also in the evening (夕). If night can be suggested by sleep, as in both these forms, then day can be transformed into night, as demonstrated by our sleepy characters shown here.

丶 亠 广 疒 疒 衤 衩 夜

开夜车	kāi yè chē	work deep into the night; burn the midnight oil
夜班	yè bān	night shift
夜半	yè bàn	midnight
夜长梦多	yè cháng mèng duō	a long night is fraught with dreams – a long delay means many hitches
夜工	yè gōng	night job
夜盲	yè máng	night blindness
夜勤	yè qín	night duty
夜晚	yè wǎn	night
夜以继日	yè yǐ jì rì	day and night; round the clock

Example:

工 程 正 在 夜 以 继 日 地 进 行 。

Gōng chéng zhèng zài yè yǐ jì rì de jìn xíng

Work is going on day and night at the construction site.

MÍNG   name; fame

In the dusk (夕), man is not clearly discernible, so he identifies himself, announcing by word of mouth (口) his name: 名. And if he has a good name and reputation, he has nothing to fear. Let him draw courage from the saying: "Travelling or at home, the gentleman does not change his name."

ノ	ク	タ	夕	夕	名	名							

名不虚传	míng bù xū chuán	live up to one's reputation
名册	míng cè	register
名产	míng chǎn	famous product
名称	míng chēng	name (of a thing or organization)
名单	míng dān	name list
名贵	míng guì	famous and precious; rare
名教	míng jiào	the Confucian ethical code
名流	míng liú	distinguished personages
名牌	míng pái	famous brand
名片	míng piàn	visiting card; calling card
名声	míng shēng	reputation; repute; renown
名胜	míng shèng	a place famous for its scenery or historical relics

Example:

他 用 的 是 一 辆 名牌 的 车子 。
Tā yòng de shì yí liàng míng pái de chē zi

The car he is using is of a famous brand.

铭（銘）

MÍNG

inscribe; engrave

Name (名) on metal or gold (金) means to carve, inscribe or engrave: 金名. Because a good name is worth more than gold, it is durable, unlike the rotten one referred to in the proverb: "Decayed wood cannot be carved."

丿 𠂉 𠂉 𠂉 金 钅 钅 钅 铭 铭 铭

铭诸肺腑	míng zhū fèi fǔ	engrave on one's mind (memory); bear firmly in mind
铭感	míng gǎn	be deeply grateful
铭记	míng jì	engrave on one's mind; always remember
铭刻	míng kè	inscription; always remember
铭文	míng wén	inscription; epigraph

Example:

他 把 母 亲 的 教 诲 铭 诸 肺 腑 。
Tā bǎ mǔ qin de jiào huì míng zhū fèi fǔ

He bore his mother's teachings firmly in mind.

怨 YUÀN

hatred;
resentment

This character is based on 心 (heart), the seat of feelings. The phonetic indicates a turning away (㔾) from someone hateful, acting as if it were night (夕) and calling it a day. If such hatred or resentment leads to violence, remember the counsel: "An angry fist cannot strike a smiling face."

丿 　 ク 　 夕 　 夗 　 夗 　 怨 　 怨 　 怨 　 怨

怨不得	yuàn bu de	cannot blame
怨愤	yuàn fèn	discontent and indignation
怨恨	yuàn hèn	have a grudge against somebody; hate; resentment
怨气	yuàn qì	grievance; complaint; resentment
怨天尤人	yuàn tiān yóu rén	blame god and man — blame everyone and everything but oneself
怨言	yuàn yán	complaint; grumble

Example:

巴 士 坏 了 ， 怨 不 得 他 们 迟 到 。
Bā shì huài le　yuàn bu de tā men chí dào

The bus broke down. No wonder they were late.

60

从 (從)

CÓNG follow; from

從 represents two men (从) walking (彳) and stopping (止). In the seal form, 彳 and 止 are united into 辵 (going). The simplified form is 从 — a man following another man — a simple task, in view of the saying: "To know the truth is easy; but, ah, how difficult it is to follow it!"

丿	人	从	从									

从容 cōng róng	calm; unhurried; leisurely	从事 cóng shì	go in for; be engaged in
从此 cóng cǐ	from this time on; henceforth	从属 cóng shǔ	subordinate
从简 cóng jiǎn	conform to the principle of simplicity	从速 cóng sù	as soon as possible
从军 cóng jūn	join the army; enlist	从头 cóng tóu	from the beginning; anew
从来 cóng lái	always; at all times; all along	从小 cóng xiǎo	from childhood; as a child
从前 cóng qián	before; formerly; in the past	从中 cóng zhōng	out of; from among

Example:

我 从 来 没 有 见 过 他 。

Wǒ cóng lái méi yǒu jiàn gūo tā

I have never seen him before.

行

XÍNG   walk; go

HÁNG   shop; trade

Originally this was a pictograph of a cross-road: 卝 . Now it is a radical which combines one step with the left foot (彳) and one step with the right (亍) to suggest walk, go or travel: 行 . Since business thrives at cross-roads, 行 can apply to shop, trade or business, on the basis of the saying: "If a little money does not go out, great money will not come in."

`	`	彳	彳	行	行				

行家	háng jia	expert
行列	háng liè	ranks
行情	háng qíng	quotations (on the market); prices
行业	háng yè	trade; profession; industry
行长	háng zhǎng	president (of a bank)
行不通	xíng bu tōng	won't do or work; get nowhere
行人	xíng rén	pedestrian
行政	xíng zhèng	administration

Example:

请 问 你 是 从 事 什 么 行 业 的 ?

Qǐng wèn nǐ shì cóng shì shén me háng yè de

May I know your profession?

得

DÉ   get; obtain

彳, the radical, means step. The phonetic 帚 — to lay hands (寸) on what one has in view (見 or 旦) — signifies to obtain. However, laying hands on money is not easy: "Money comes like earth picked up with a pin, but goes like sand washed away by water."

丿 丿 彳 彳 彳 彳 彳 得 得 得 得

得寸进尺	dé cùn jìn chǐ	give him an inch and he"ll take an ell; be insatiable
得到	dé dào	get; obtain; gain; receive
得分	dé fēn	score
得奖	dé jiǎng	win or be awarded a prize
得胜	dé shèng	win a victory; triumph
得失	dé shī	gain and loss; success and failure

得势	dé shì	be in power; get the upper hand
得悉	dé xī	hear of; learn about
得益	dē yì	benefit; profit
得志	dé zhì	achieve one's ambition
得罪	dé zuì	offend; displease

Example:

两 种 办 法 各 有 得 失 。
Liáng zhǒng bàn fǎ gè yǒu dé shī
Each of the two methods has its advantages and disadvantages.

63

德

DÉ

virtue; goodness

直 means straight (〜) as tested by ten (十) eyes (目). 心 is the heart. So the phonetic 悳 denotes a straight heart. Clarified by the radical for step (彳) to mean the way to virtue or goodness, 德 is defined by the saying: "To talk good is not being good; to do good, that is being good."

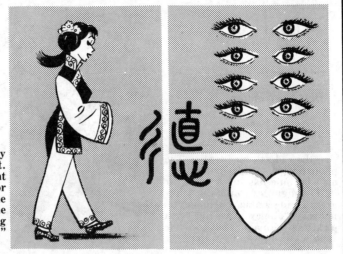

PENG

丿 彳 彳 彳 彳 彳 徝 徝 徝 徝 德 德 德 德 德

德高望重	dé gāo wàng zhòng	be of noble character and high prestige
德国	Dé Guó	Germany
德行	dé xíng	moral integrity; moral conduct
德育	dé yù	moral education
品德	pǐn dé	moral character

Example:

政 府 现 在 正 在 积 极 推 行 德 育 。
Zhèng fǔ xiàn zài zhèng zài jī jí tuī xíng dé yù

The government is at present actively promoting moral education.

徒

TÚ

follower;
go on foot

The seal form of 走 is 孟 — a man bending forward (大) to go on foot, (止) i.e., walk. The seal form of 徒 , however, is 社 — one who goes (辵) on the ground,(土) i.e., a disciple who walks in the footsteps of his master, like the shadow following the substance.

| ノ | ク | オ | 彳 | 彳 | 彳 | 彳 | 往 | 待 | 徒 | 徒 |

徒步	tú bù	on foot
徒弟	tú dì	apprentice; disciple
徒工	tú gōng	apprentice
徒劳	tú láo	futile effort; fruitless labour

Example:

他 已 尽 了 力 ， 到 最 后 还 是 徒 劳 无 功 。
Tā yǐ jìn le lì   dào zuì hòu hái shì tú láo wú gōng
He has tried his best but to no avail.

HĚN

very;
quite

The phonetic 艮 (originally 㫔) means stubborn — to turn around (ヒ)and eye (目) another defiantly. The radical 彳 (step) suggests the steps needed to curb this stubbornness; hence intensive, very. An analogous character is 狠 — obstinate (艮) and beastly (犭).

ノ	ク	彳	彳コ	彳ヨ	彳ヨ	彳艮	很	很				

好得很   hǎo de hěn   very good

很有道理   hěn yǒu dào li   contain much truth; be quite correct

Example:

他 的 上 司 对 他 的 工 作 表 现 感 到 很 满 意 。

Tā de shàng si duì tā de gōng zuò biǎo xiàn gǎn dào hěn mǎn yì

His boss is very pleased with his work performance.

街 **JIĒ** road; street

行, the radical, represents footprints; it means to go, walk or travel. The phonetic 圭 (soil 土 doubled) suggests road, street or ground for walking. Travelling on a road can be trying, hence: "Long roads test the horse; long dealings test the friend."

ノ ク イ 彳 彳 彳 往 往 往 往 街 街

街道	jiē dào		street; residential district; neighbourhood
街坊	jiē fang		neighbour
街市	jiē shì		downtown streets
街头	jiē tóu		street corner; street
街头巷尾	jiē tóu xiàng wěi		streets and lanes

Example:

街 头 巷 尾 ， 到 处 都 是 欢 乐 的 人 群 。
Jiē tóu xiàng wěi   dào chù dōu shì huān lè   de rén qún

There are happy crowds in all the streets and lanes.

67

LÜ

律

law; rule
discipline

The phonetic 聿 signifies written regulations — hand (彐) with pen (丨) writing lines (一) on tablet (一). The radical 彳 (step) suggests steps taken to enforce them as law to protect the citizens. However, "Going to the law is losing a cow for the sake of a cat."

ノ　ノ　彳　彳　彳　彳　律　律　律

律吕	lǜ lǚ	bamboo pitch-pipes used in ancient China; temperament
律师	lǜ shī	lawyer; barrister; solicitor
律诗	lǜ shī	a poem of eight lines, each containing five or seven characters, with a strict tonal pattern and rhyme scheme

Example:

辩 方 律 师 为 被 告 辩 护 。

Biàn fāng lǜ shī wèi bèi gào biàn hù

The lawyer speaks in defence of the accused.

HOU
after; behind

This character combines three signs: 彳 (step with left foot), 幺 (the finest thread, least or last) and 夂 (hindered at the feet from behind). All three factors contribute to the sense: behind, after or future. 後 is now simplified to 后 (empress) probably because the queen goes after the king in traditional China.

PENG

ノ	厂	厂	斤	后	后									

后半	hòu bàn	latter half; second half
后备军	hòu bèi jūn	reserves; reserve force
后辈	hòu bèi	younger generation; posterity
后代	hòu dài	later periods (in history)
后方	hòu fāng	rear
后跟	hòu gēn	heel (of a shoe or sock)
后果	hòu guǒ	consequence; aftermath

后患	hòu huàn	future trouble
后悔	hòu huǐ	regret; repent
后会有期	hòu huì yǒu qī	we'll meet again some day
后景	hòu jǐng	background
后来	hòu lái	afterwards; later
后天	hòu tiān	day after tomorrow; postnatal; acquired

Example:

知 识 是 后 天 获 得 的 ，　不 是 先 天 就 有 的 。
Zhī shi shì hòu tiān huò dé de　bú shì xiān tiān jiù yǒu de
Knowledge is acquired, not innate.

DÀI

treat; deal with

寺 is a court where the law or rule
(寸) is applied continually, like the
growth of a plant (⼟). The radical
彳 indicates the step or way to treat
others with propriety, requiring pa-
tience and application of the golden
rule: "Do to others as you would
have them do to you."

丿 彳 彳 彳 彳 往 往 待 待

| | | | |

待命　　　　dài mìng　　　　await orders
待人接物　　dài rén jiē wù　　the way one gets along with people
待续　　　　dài xù　　　　　to be continued
待遇　　　　dài yù　　　　　treatment; remuneration

Example:

这 间 公 司 对 职 员 很 照 顾 ， 给 的 待 遇 也 很 好 。
Zhè jiān gōng sī duì zhí yuán hěn zhào gu　gěi de dài yù yě hěn hǎo
This company treats its employees well, and also offers attractive remuneration.

70

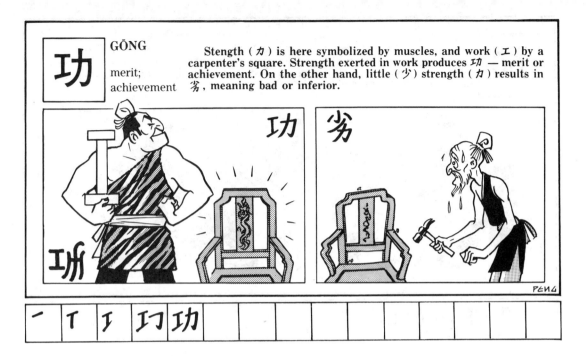

功 GŌNG

merit; achievement

Stength (力) is here symbolized by muscles, and work (工) by a carpenter's square. Strength exerted in work produces 功 — merit or achievement. On the other hand, little (少) strength (力) results in 劣, meaning bad or inferior.

一 丁 工 功 功

功败垂成	gōng bài chuí chéng	fail in a great undertaking on the verge of success
功德	gōng dé	merits and virtues
功课	gōng kè	schoolwork; homework
功亏一篑	gōng kuī yī kuì	fall short of success for lack of a final effort
功劳	gōng láo	contribution; meritorious service; credit
功能	gōng néng	function
功效	gōng xiào	efficacy; effect

Example:

她 的 功 劳 可 不 小 啊 ！

Tā de gōng lao kě bù xiǎo ǎ

She has certainly made no small contribution!

71

JIĀ

add;
increase

This ideograph means to add to or increase. It adds strength (力) to mouth (口) by applying force to words. Adding violence to persuasion cannot always be justified. Although might is never right, right is always might.

PENG

| 丁 | 力 | 加 | 加 | 加 | | | | | | | | |

加班	jiā bān	work overtime
加倍	jiā bèi	double; redouble
加法	jiā fǎ	addition
加害	jiā hài	injure; do harm to
加紧	jiā jǐn	step up; speed up; intensify
加宽	jiā kuān	broaden; widen
加仑	jiā lún	gallon

加冕	jiā miǎn	coronation
加强	jiā qiáng	strengthen; enhance
加入	jiā rù	add; mix; join; accede to
加速	jiā sù	accelerate; expedite
加意	jiā yì	with special care; with close attention
加油	jiā yóu	refuel; make an extra effort

Example:

观 众 为 运 动 员 们 加 油 。
Guān zhòng wèi yùn dòng yuán men jiā yóu
The spectators cheered the players on.

72

办 (辦)

BÀN handle; manage

辛 is one who has offended (丮) a superior (宀 or 上). 勃辛 means to handle or manage; literally, to interpose force (力) between two offenders (辛辛). Such man-handling often leads to injury. Better to heed the proverb: "Just scales and full measure injure no man."

フ	カ	劝	办								

办案	bàn àn	handle a case
办到	bàn dào	get something done; accomplish
办法	bàn fǎ	way; means; measure
办公	bàn gōng	handle official business; work (usually in an office)
办理	bàn lǐ	handle; conduct; transact
办事	bàn shì	handle affairs; work
办罪	bàn zuì	punish

Example:

这 些 事 情 你 可 以 斟 酌 办 理 。
Zhè xiē shì qing ni kě yi zhēn zhuó bàn li
You may handle these matters as you see fit.

73

协 (協)

XIÉ

together;
co-operate

Triple-strength (劦), signifying the multiple efforts of ten (十) persons in unity, indicates wholehearted cooperation: 協. Without cooperation, shared responsibility leads to neglect. "If two men feed a horse, it will be thin, if two men mend a boat, it will leak."

PENG

| 一 | 十 | 忄丁 | 协 | 协 | 协 | | | | | | | |

协定	xié dìng	agreement; accord		协同	xié tóng	work in coordination with; cooperate with
协会	xié huì	association; society		协议	xié yì	agree on; agreement
协力	xié lì	unite efforts; join in a common effort		协助	xié zhù	assist; help; give assistance
协商	xié shāng	consult; talk things over		协奏曲	xié zòu qǔ	concerto
协调	xié tiáo	coordinate; concert; harmonize		协作	xié zuò	cooperation; coordination; combined

Example:

体 操 运 动 员 的 动 作 协 调 优 美 。

Tǐ cāo yùn dòng yuán de dòng zuò xié tiáo yōu měi

The gymnast's movements are harmonious and graceful.

劳 (勞)

LÁO　work; labour

勞 is to toil (力) indoors (宀) by the light of many fires (火火). Burning the midnight oil or the candle at both ends is a waste of effort. "It is labour lost, trying to catch the moon in the water or polishing brick to make a mirror."

一　十　艹　艹　芦　芦　劳

劳动	láo dòng	work; labour
劳而无功	láo ér wú gōng	work hard but to no avail
劳工	láo gōng	labourer; worker
劳累	láo lèi	tired; run-down
劳力	láo lì	labour; labour force
劳碌	láo lù	work hard; toil

劳神	láo shén	be a tax on (one's mind); bother; trouble
劳心	láo xīn	work with one's mind or brains
劳燕分飞	láo yàn fēn fēi	part; separate
劳资	láo zī	labour and capital

Example:

你 现 在 身 体 不 好 ， 不 要 过 于 劳 神 。

Nǐ xiàn zài shēn tǐ bù hǎo 　 bù yào guò yú láo shén

You're in poor health; so don't overtax yourself.

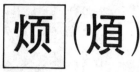

烦 (煩)

FÁN troubled; irritated

頁 refers to the head (百) upon a body (儿). 火 , the radical, represents fire or fever. When you are grieved or irritated, with fire in the head, remember: "Though starving to death, do not steal; though annoyed to death, do not file a lawsuit."

PENG

丶　丶丶　少　火　灯　灯　灯　炳　烦　烦

烦闷	fán mèn	be unhappy; be worried
烦恼	fán nǎo	be vexed; be worried
烦扰	fán rǎo	feel disturbed
烦冗	fán rǒng	(of one's affairs) diverse and complicated; (of speech or writing) lengthy and tedious
烦燥	fán zào	be fidgety; be agitated

Example:

某 些 动 物 烦 燥 不 安 可 能 是 地 震 临 震 前 的 预 兆 。

Mǒu xiē dòng wù fán zào bù ān kě néng shì dì zhèn lín zhèn qián de yù zhào

Agitated activity by certain animals may be a sign of an impending earthquake.

76

光 **GUĀNG**

light;
glory

The ancient form 荧 means twenty (廿) fires (火). The modern form 炎 portrays a man (儿) bearing a torch (火). Whatever the form, 光 means brightness and glory which, unfortunately, never lasts. Hence: "A bright dawn does not always make a fine day."

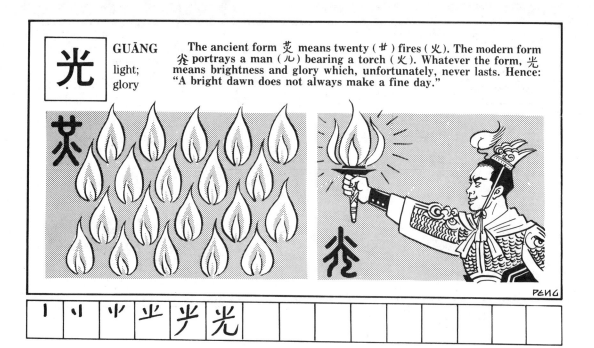

丨 丬 屮 业 半 光

光彩	guāng cǎi	lustre; splendour; radiance; honourable; glorious
光辐射	guāng fú shè	ray radiation
光顾	guāng gù	patronize
光棍儿	guāng gùn er	unmarried man; bachelor
光辉	guāng huī	radiance; brilliance
光景	guāng jǐng	scene; circumstances
光芒万丈	guāng máng wàn zhàng	shining with boundless radiance
光明	guāng míng	light; bright; promising
光荣	guāng róng	honour; glory; credit
光天化日	guāng tiān huà rì	broad daylight

Example:

光 彩 绚 丽 的 贝 雕 吸 引 了 许 多 观 众 。
Guāng cǎi xuàn lì de bèi diāo xī yǐn le xǔ duō guān zhòng
The brilliant lustre of the shell attracted many visitors.

先

XIĀN

first;
before

The top part 生 is a small plant (Ψ) issuing from the ground (一); thus indicating progress. The lower part is a picture of marching legs. Accordingly, 先 means to advance (生) on one's feet (ㄦ) — to be first. And to progress with people, remember: "Courtesy first, force later" (先礼后兵).

PENG

丿 ㇒ 丰 生 生 先

先辈	xiān bèi	elder generation; ancestors
先导	xiān dǎo	guide; forerunner
先后	xiān hòu	early or late; priority; one after another
先进	xiān jìn	advanced
先来后到	xiān lái hòu dào	first come, first served
先生	xiān sheng	teacher; mister
先下手为强	xiān xià shǒu wéi qiáng	he who strikes first gains the advantage
先知	xiān zhī	person of foresight; prophet

Example:

这 些 事 都 该 办 ； 可 也 得 有 个 先 后 。
Zhè xiē shì dōu gāi bàn kě yě děi yǒu gè xiān hòu

All these matters should be tackled, but they should be taken up in order of priority.

78

洗

XǏ wash; clean

The radical is 氵 (water) and the phonetic 先 (first). This suggests that you must have water (氵) first (先) to wash or clean: 洗. And what needs to be cleansed first? According to the proverbial exhortation: "Cleanse your heart as you would cleanse a dish."

丶 丶 氵 氵 氵 氵 氵 氵 洗

洗尘	xǐ chén	give a dinner of welcome (to a visitor from afar)
洗涤	xǐ dí	wash; cleanse
洗发剂	xǐ fà jì	shampoo
洗劫	xǐ jié	loot; sack
洗刷	xǐ shuā	wash and brush; scrub
洗心革面	xǐ xīn gé miàn	turn over a new leaf
洗印	xǐ yìn	developing and printing; processing
洗澡	xǐ zǎo	have a bath; bathe

Example:

新 年 到 了 ， 大 家 忙 着 洗 刷 屋 子 和 房 间 。
Xīn nián dào le　　dà jiā máng zhe xǐ shuā wū zi hé fáng jiān
Everybody is busy washing and cleaning the house in preparation for the coming new year.

波 BŌ
waves; ripples

The saying goes: "When there is wind in the clouds, there are waves on the river." Such waves (波) appear on the surface and are likened to the skin (皮) of water (氵). When waves (波) of wrinkles appear on the skin of a woman (女), we have 婆 — an old woman.

丶 氵 氵 汀 沪 沪 波 波

波长	bō cháng	wavelength	
波荡	bō dàng	heave; surge	
波段	bō duàn	wave band	
波兰	Bō Lán	Poland	
波浪	bō làng	wave	

波涛	bō tāo	great waves; billows
波纹	bō wén	ripple; corrugation
波折	bō zhé	twists and turns
物价波动	wù jià bō dòng	price fluctuation

Example:

事 情 发 生 了 波 折 。
Shì qing fā shēng le bō zhé
Events took an unexpected turn.

海 HǍI

sea; ocean

母 is a picture of a woman with breasts for suckling a child, signifying mother (母).

每 compares a mother (母) with a sprout (丿), always reproducing; hence meaning every, always.

海 represents the sea, where there is always (每) plenty of water (氵)

丶 丶丶 氵 氵 氵 汽 海 海 海 海

海岸	hǎi àn	coast; seashore
海豹	hǎi bào	seal
海滨	hǎi bīn	seaside
海产	hǎi chǎn	marine products
海盗	hǎi dào	pirate; sea rover
海港	hǎi gǎng	seaport; harbour
海关检查	hǎi guān jiǎn chá	customs inspection
海军	hǎi jūn	navy

海枯石烂	hǎi kū shí làn	(even if) the seas run dry and the rocks crumble
海上	hǎi shàng	at sea; on the sea
海外	hǎi wài	overseas; abroad
海湾	hǎi wān	bay; gulf
海峡	hǎi xiá	strait; channel
海鲜	hǎi xiān	seafood
海员	hǎi yuán	seaman; sailor; mariner

Example:

海 枯 石 烂 心 不 变 。

Hǎi kū shí làn xīn bù biàn

The sea may run dry and the rocks may crumble, but our hearts will alway remain loyal.

81

渴

KĚ thirsty

The phonetic 曷 is to ask; literally, a beggar (勾) who speaks (曰). 勾 itself means a wanderer (勹) who seeks to enter (入) a refuge (乚). 曰 is a mouth (口) with word (一). When you ask (曷) for water (氵) you must be thirsty: 渴. "When you are thirsty, a drop of water can be likened to a sweet dew."

PENG

`丶  丶丶  氵  氵` 氿 沪 沪 沪 渴 渴 渴

渴望	kě wàng	thirst for; long for; yearn for
渴念	kě niàn	miss very much
渴睡	kě shuì	a cat nap; to doze; sleepy
渴仰	kě yǎng	adore; admire

Example:

许 多 青 年 渴 望 参 加 空 军。

Xǔ duō qīng nián kě wàng cān jiā kōng jūn

Many young people long to join the Air Force.

法 FǍ

law; statute

Water is essential to life and benefits everybody. Laws are also meant to benefit every citizen. Just as water (氵) removes (去) dirt, so the law (法) smoothens morals by removing vices. However, never resort to law; if you win, you lose; and if you lose, you're lost.

丶 冫 氵 氵 汁 法 法 法

法案	fǎ àn	proposed law; bill
法宝	fǎ bǎo	a magic weapon
法定	fǎ dìng	legal; statutory
法定人数	fǎ dìng rén shù	quorum
法官	fǎ guān	judge; justice
法规	fǎ guī	laws and regulations
法令	fǎ lìng	laws and decrees

法律	fǎ lǜ	law; statute
法庭	fǎ tíng	court; tribunal
法网	fǎ wǎng	the net of justice; the arm of the law
法西斯	fǎ xī sī	fascist
法子	fǎ zi	way; method

Example:

我 们 得 想 个 法 子 解 决 这 个 问 题 。
Wǒ men dé xiǎng gè fǎ zi jiě jué zhè ge wèn tí
We'll have to think of a way to solve the problem.

LÍN

forest

"A single fibre does not make a thread; a single tree does not make a forest," so goes the saying. The character for tree is a pictograph: 木. Two trees form a company — a grove or forest: 林. Three trees make a crowd, signifying dense or overgrown: 森.

一 十 才 木 朩 村 材 林

艺林	yì lín	art circles
竹林	zhú lín	bamboo grove
林产品	lín chǎn pǐn	forest products
林带	lín dài	forest belt
林立	lín lì	stand in great numbers (like trees in a forest)
林木	lín mù	forest; woods
林荫道	lín yīn dào	boulevard; avenue

Example:

港 口 樯 桅 林 立 。
Gǎng kǒu qiáng wéi lín lì

There is a forest of masts in the harbour.

84

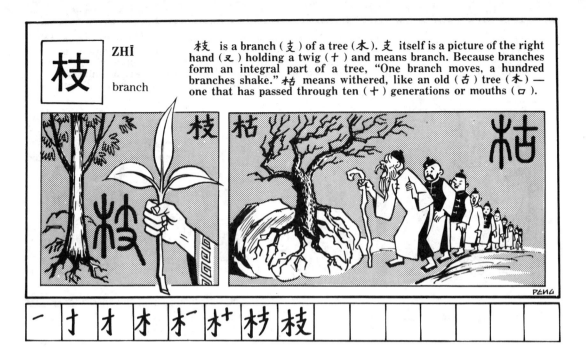

枝 **ZHĪ**

branch

枝 is a branch (支) of a tree (木). 支 itself is a picture of the right hand (又) holding a twig (十) and means branch. Because branches form an integral part of a tree, "One branch moves, a hundred branches shake." 枯 means withered, like an old (古) tree (木) — one that has passed through ten (十) generations or mouths (口).

一　十　才　才　才　才　杉　枝

枝杈	*zhī chà*	branch; twig
枝接	*zhī jiē*	scion grafting
枝节	*zhī jié*	branches and knots – minor matters; complication; unexpected difficulty
枝叶	*zhī yè*	branches and leaves; non-essentials
枝子	*zhī zi*	branch; twig

Example:

不 要 过 多 地 注 意 那 些 枝 枝 节 节 。
Bú yào gūo duō de zhù yì nà xiē zhī zhī jié jié
Don't pay too much attention to the minor issues.

85

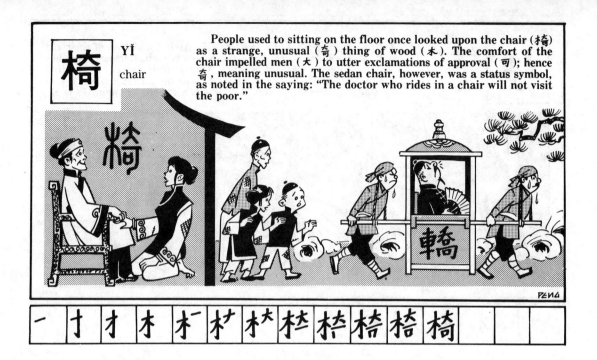

椅 YǏ
chair

People used to sitting on the floor once looked upon the chair (椅) as a strange, unusual (奇) thing of wood (木). The comfort of the chair impelled men (大) to utter exclamations of approval (可); hence 奇, meaning unusual. The sedan chair, however, was a status symbol, as noted in the saying: "The doctor who rides in a chair will not visit the poor."

| 椅子 | yǐ zi | chair |
| 椅子頂 | yǐ zi dǐng | balancing on a pyramid of chairs |

Example:

他 家 很 贫 穷 ， 连 椅 子 也 没 有 。
Tā jiā hěn pín qióng lián yǐ zi yě méi yǒu
He was so very poor that he had no chairs in his house.

楼 (樓)

LÓU
storey

The phonetic 婁 refers to the part of a palace where women (女) are enclosed (中) and confined (母). The addition of the tree radical (木) suggests a tower high as a tree and one with several floors: 樓.

一 十 才 才 才 才 杉 杜 村 杵 楼 楼 楼

楼板	lóu bǎn	floor; floorslab
楼房	lóu fáng	a building of two or more storeys
楼上	lóu shàng	upstairs
楼台	lóu tái	a high building; tower; balcony
楼梯	lóu tī	stairs; staircase
楼下	lóu xià	downstairs

Example:

楼 上 住 的 是 一 位 退 休 老 工 人 。
Lóu shàng zhù de shì yī wèi tuì xiū lǎo gōng rén
A retired worker lives upstairs.

87

病 病

BÌNG sickness

The radical for disease 疒 (疒) is made up of a horizontal line (−) — the position of a sick person — and the bed (爿). The idea of sickness is reinforced by the phonetic 丙 (疾) — fire (火) in the house (宀), referring to high fever. 病 also means defect or fault, and it is said: "A wise doctor never treats himself."

| 丶 | 一 | 广 | 疒 | 疒 | 疒 | 疒 | 病 | 病 | 病 | | | | |

流行病	líu xíng bìng	epidemic disease
心脏病	xīn zàng bìng	heart trouble; heart disease
病从口入	bìng cóng kǒu rù	illness finds its way in by the mouth
病倒	bìng dǎo	be down with an illness; be laid up
病假	bìng jià	sick leave
病况	bìng kuàng	state of an illness; patient's condition
病态	bìng tài	morbid state
病痛	bìng tòng	slight illness; indisposition; ailment

Example:

他 犯 错 误 的 病 根 在 于 私 心 太 重 。
Tā fàn cuò wù de bìng gēn zài yú sī xīn tài zhòng
His error stems from selfishness.

TÉNG   pain; ache

Just as fire or fever suggests sickness, winter (冬) or intense cold is here combined with the radical for sickness (疒) to signify pain: 疼. However, young and old do not feel pain alike. In youth, the absence of pleasure is pain; in old age, the absence of pain is pleasure.

丶 亠 广 疒 疒 疒 疒 疒 疼 疼

疼爱	téng ài	be very fond of; love dearly
疼痛	téng tòng	pain; ache; soreness

Example:

婆 婆 最 疼 小 孙 子 。

Pó po zuì téng xiǎo sūn zi

Granny dotes on her little grandson.

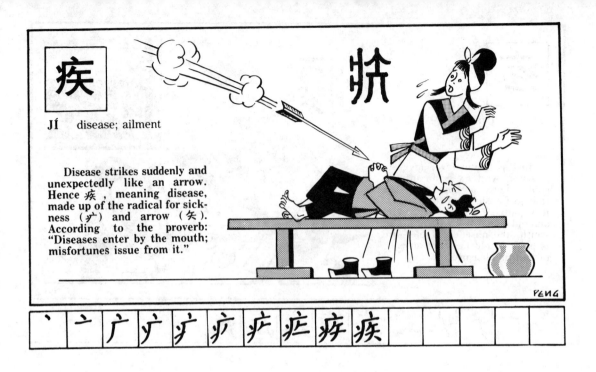

疾

Jí   disease; ailment

Disease strikes suddenly and unexpectedly like an arrow. Hence 疾, meaning disease, made up of the radical for sickness (疒) and arrow (矢). According to the proverb: "Diseases enter by the mouth; misfortunes issue from it."

、　一　广　疒　疒　疒　疒　疒　疾　疾

眼疾	yǎn jí	eye trouble
疾病	jí bìng	disease; illness
疾风	jí fēng	strong wind; gale
疾苦	jí kǔ	sufferings; hardships
疾言厉色	jí yán lì sè	harsh words and stern looks

Example:

他 对 人 很 和 蔼 ， 从 不 疾 言 厉 色 。
Tā duì rén hěn hé ǎi cóng bù jí yán lì sè
He is affable and is never brusque with people.

90

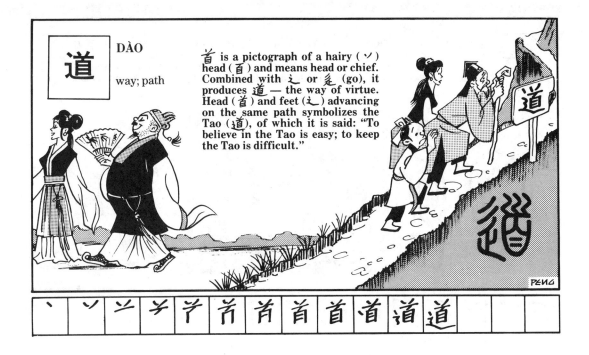

道　DÀO
way; path

首 is a pictograph of a hairy (㇒) head (百) and means head or chief. Combined with 辶 or 辵 (go), it produces 道 — the way of virtue. Head (首) and feet (辶) advancing on the same path symbolizes the Tao (道), of which it is said: "To believe in the Tao is easy; to keep the Tao is difficult."

`丶` `丷` `ソ` `丷` `丷` `䒑` `首` `首` `首` `首` `道` `道`

道德	dào dé	morals; morality; ethics	
道贺	dào hè	congratulate	
道教	Dào Jiào	Taoism	
道具	dào jù	stage property; prop	
道理	dào li	principle; truth; hows and whys; reason; sense	

道路	dào lù	road; way; path
道歉	dào qiàn	apologize; make an apology
道士	dào shi	Taoist priest
道喜	dào xǐ	congratulate somebody on a happy occasion
道谢	dào xiè	express one's thanks; thank

Example:

你 的 话 很 有 道 理 。
Nǐ de huà hěn yǒu dào li
What you said is quite reasonable.

91

面 MIÀN

face

This radical incorporates 囗, an outline of the face, with 百 (head) featuring the eyes (目) as its most prominent part. Because a person is identified by his face, we know a man's face, not his mind. Nevertheless, "Be able to say in his face what you say behind his back."

一 ｢ ｢ 丆 而 而 面 面

面对	miàn duì	face; confront
面对面	miàn duì miàn	facing each other; face-to-face
面粉	miàn fěn	wheat flour; flour
面红耳赤	miàn hóng ěr chì	be flushed
面积	miàn ji	area
面颊	miàn jiá	cheek

面具	miàn jù	mask
面貌	miàn mào	face; features
面目	miàn mù	face; features; look; aspect
面前	miàn qián	in front of; before
面熟	mià shú	look familiar
面条	miàn tiáo	noodles
面子	miàn zi	reputation; prestige; face

Example:

展 览 会 面 积 为 三 千 平 方 米 。

Zhǎn lǎn huì miàn ji wéi sān qiān píng fāng mǐ

The exhibition covers a floor space of 3000 square metres.

瞎

XIĀ   blind

瞎 stands for injured (害) eyes (目). The phonetic 害 (harm) represents injury from a stick (丨) with notches (三) or injury by mouth (口) under cover (宀).

Another ideograph for blind is 盲 or lost (亡) eyes (目). Despite their handicap, "The blind are quick at hearing; the deaf are quick at sight."

PENG

丨 冂 冂 月 目 目ˋ 目ˊ 目宀 目宀 目宀 目宀 瞎 瞎 瞎 瞎

瞎扯	xiā chě	talk irresponsibly; talk rubbish
瞎话	xiā huà	untruth; lie
瞎闹	xiā nào	act senselessly; mess about; fool around; be mischievous
瞎说	xiā shuō	talk irresponsibly; talk rubbish
瞎子	xiā zi	a blind person

Example:

赶 快 做 作 业 ， 别 瞎 闹 。

Gǎn kuài zuò zuò yè   bié xiā nào

Do your homework quickly and don't fool around.

93

SHUÌ

睡

sleep

睡 is to have the eyes or eyelids (目) hanging down (垂) — to sleep. The phonetic 垂 or 坙 depicts a bough loaded with leaves (𠂹) hanging down towards the earth (土). Sleep, even if your eyes are closed, is not always a peaceful affair. According to the saying, "Attending to the Emperor is like sleeping with a tiger."

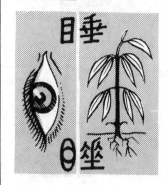

丨 冂 冂 月 目 目′ 目′ 目′ 目′ 目′ 目′ 睡 睡

睡觉	shuì jiào	sleep
睡莲	shuì lián	water lily
睡梦	shuì mèng	sleep; slumber
睡眠	shuì mián	sleep
睡醒	shuì xǐng	wake up
睡衣	shuì yī	night clothes; pyjamas
睡意	shuì yì	sleepiness; drowsiness

Example:

一 阵 敲 门 声 把 他 从 睡 梦 中 惊 醒 了 。

Yī zhèn qiāo mén shēng bǎ tā cóng shuì mèng zhōng jīng xǐng le

He was roused from sleep by a heavy pounding on the door.

94

发 (髮)

FÀ　hair

The seal form of the radical 髟 is 髟. It depicts long hair (彡) tied with a band (一) and pinned with a brooch (ㄨ). Three strokes are added to emphasize the locks (彡). The phonetic 犮 or 犮 is a dog led by a leash — an allusion to the practice of leading underdogs by the hair.

ㄥ　ㄐ　ㄅ　发　发

理发	lǐ fà	haircut	
发型	fà xíng	hair style; hairdo	
发表	fā biǎo	publish; issue	
发财	fā cái	get rich; make a fortune	
发愁	fā chóu	worry; be anxious	
发达	fā dá	developed; flourishing	
发动	fā dòng	start; launch; mobilize	
发抖	fā dǒu	shiver; shake; tremble	

发愤	fā fèn	make a firm resolution
发慌	fā huāng	feel nervous; get flustered
发觉	fā jué	find; detect; discover
发明	fā míng	invent
发生	fā shēng	happen; occur; take place
发售	fā shòu	sell; put on sale
发言权	fā yán quán	right to speak
发展	fā zhǎn	develop; expand; grow

Example:

那 里 发 生 了 强 烈 地 震 。
Nà lǐ fā shēng le qiáng liè dì zhèn
A violent earthquake occurred there.

WÈI   stomach

This ideograph combines two pictographs. The upper one is a pouch filled with rice: ⊗ ; the lower, a piece of flesh: 月 . Hence, stomach — a fleshy pouch filled with rice. Although a full stomach begets a contented mind, "Better be hungry and pure than well-filled and corrupt."

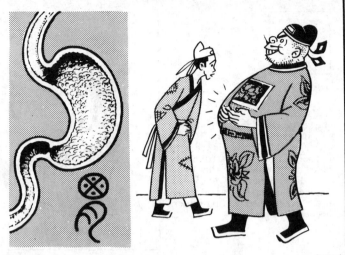

丶　冂　冃　甲　田　胃　胃　胃　胃

胃病	wèi bìng	stomach trouble; gastric disease
胃口	wèi kǒu	appetite; liking
胃溃疡	wèi kuì yáng	gastric ulcer
胃酸	wèi suān	hydrochloric acid in gastric juice
胃痛	wèi tòng	gastralgia
胃液	wèi yè	gastric juice

Example:

她 的 胃 口 很 好 ， 吃 了 很 多 。

Tā   de   wèi   kǒu   hěn   hǎo   chī   le   hěn   duō

She was eating a lot because she had a very good appetite.

思

SĪ think

This ideograph combines the skull (⊗) with the heart (♨) to produce thought: 思 . The faculties of reasoning and feeling are here exercised to create a balanced mind. And, according to the saying, "If you wish to know the mind of a man, listen to his words."

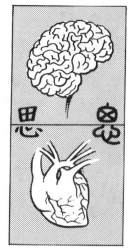

PENG

丶　冂　冂　甲　田　田　思　思　思

思潮	sī cháo	trend of thought; ideological trend; thoughts
思考	sī kǎo	think deeply; ponder over; reflect on
思念	sī niàn	think of; long for; miss
思索	sī suǒ	think deeply; ponder
思想	sī xiǎng	thought; thinking; idea; ideology

Example:

我 一 夜 没 睡 着 ， 反 复 思 索 这 个 问 题 。
Wǒ yī yè méi shuì zháo   fǎn fù sī suǒ zhè ge wèn tí
I lay awake all night, turning the problem over and over in my mind.

情	QÍNG
	feeling; affection

弄 is green — the colour (丹) of nature and growing plants (生). With the addition of the radical for heart (忄) the character stands for those feelings which are pure or natural to the heart of man: 情. Lamenting the lack of depth and substance in such feelings, the saying goes: "Human feelings are as thin as sheets of paper."

丶 丷 忄 忄¯ 忄= 忄丰 忭 情 情 情

情报	qíng bào	intelligence; information	情节	qíng jié	plot; circumstances
情不自禁	qíng bù zì jìn	be seized with a sudden impulse to	情况	qíng kuàng	circumstances; situation
情操	qíng cāo	sentiment	情理	qíng lǐ	reason; sense
情敌	qíng dí	rival in love	情侣	qíng lǚ	sweethearts; lovers
情调	qíng diào	sentiment; emotional appeal	情趣	qíng qù	temperament and interest
情窦初开	qíng dòu chū kāi	(of a young girl) first awakening of love	情绪	qíng xù	morale; feeling; mood; sentiments
情感	qíng gǎn	emotion; feeling	情愿	qíng yuàn	be willing to; would rather

Example:

这 个 剧 本 情 节 很 复 杂 。
Zhè ge jù běn qíng jié hěn fù zá
The play has a very complicated plot.

<table>
<tr><td>拜</td><td>**BÀI**

salute
respect;</td><td>拜, to pay respects to man or god, was first written as 𦥑, depicting two hands (𦥑) hanging down (下 or 丅) in salutation or worship. With respect to worship, it has been said: "He who lives near the temple ridicules the gods." Also: "Far better it is to be respectful at home than to burn incense in a far place."</td></tr>
</table>

ノ ニ 三 手 手 手 拝 拝 拜 拜

拜别	bài bié	take leave of
拜倒	bài dǎo	prostrate oneself; fall on one's knees
拜访	bài fǎng	pay a visit
拜见	bài jiàn	pay a formal visit; call to pay respects
拜年	bài nián	pay a New Year call
拜寿	bài shòu	congratulate an elderly person on his birthday
拜托	bài tuō	request somebody to do something

Example:

姑 妈 ， 我 们 给 您 拜 年 来 啦 ！
Gū mā   wǒ men gěi nín bài nián lái la

Auntie, we've come to wish you a Happy New Year.

99

FÀNG

release

放 means to release — to drive out (攵) into an open space or pasture (方). The radical 攵 (攴) is a hand with stick; the phonetic 方 is a square or open space. Horses or cattle released for grazing can always be rounded up, but "Words once released cannot be recaptured by the swiftest steeds."

丶 亠 方 方 放 放 放

放出	fàng chū	give out; let out; emit
放大	fàng dà	enlarge; magnify; amplify
放胆	fàng dǎn	act boldly and with confidence
放荡	fàng dàng	dissolute; dissipated
放工	fàng gōng	(of workers) knock off
放火	fàng huǒ	set fire to; set on fire
放假	fàng jià	have a vacation; have a day off
放宽	fàng kuān	relax restrictions; relax

放弃	fàng qì	abandon; give up; renounce
放下	fàng xià	lay down; put down
放心	fàng xīn	set one's mind at rest
放学	fàng xué	classes are over
放映	fàng yìng	show; project
放置	fàng zhì	lay up; lay aside
放逐	fàng zhú	send into exile; banish

Example:

你 放 心 ， 一 切 都 会 安 排 好 的 。
Nǐ fàng xīn　yī qiè dōu huì ān pái hǎo de
You can rest assured that everything will be all right.

100

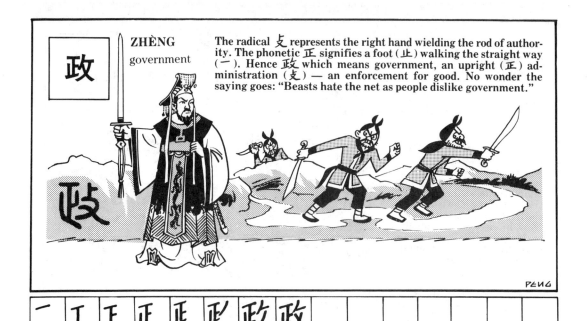

ZHÈNG

government

政

The radical 攵 represents the right hand wielding the rod of authority. The phonetic 正 signifies a foot (止) walking the straight way (一). Hence 政 which means government, an upright (正) administration (攵) — an enforcement for good. No wonder the saying goes: "Beasts hate the net as people dislike government."

一 丁 下 正 正 卫 政 政

政变	zhèng biàn	coup d'etat	
政策	zhèng cè	policy	
政党	zhèng dǎng	political party	
政敌	zhèng dí	political opponent	
政法	zhèng fǎ	politics and law	
政府	zhèng fǔ	government	
政界	zhèng jiè	political circles; government circles	
政局	zhèng jú	political situation; political scene	
政客	zhèng kè	politician	
政权	zhèng quán	political power; regime	
政治	zhèng zhì	politics; political affairs	

Example:

哥 哥 在 政 府 部 门 工 作 。

Gē ge zài zhèng fǔ bù mén gōng zuō

My elder brother works in the civil service.

菜 CÀI

vegetable

菜, the character for vegetables, is made up of 艹 and 采. The radical for grass (艹) suggests a small plant. 采, the phonetic, shows the right hand (爫) reaching down to pluck the fruit of a plant or tree (木). How often we have plucked such fruit, thinking nothing of the tree that bore it and the One who made it grow!

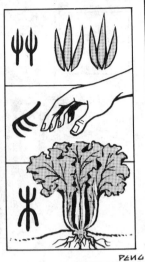

PENG

一　十　艹　艹　芐　芣　芣　苹　芣　茅　菜

菜场	cài chǎng	food market
菜单	cài dān	menu
菜花	cài huā	cauliflower
菜农	cài nóng	vegetable grower
菜市	cài shì	food market
菜蔬	cài shū	vegetables
菜园	cài yuán	vegetable garden; vegetable farm

Example:

舅　母　的　家　后　面　有　一　小　片　菜　园　。
Jiù mǔ de jiā hòu mian yǒu yì xiǎo piàn cài yuán

My aunt has a small plot of vegetable garden at the back of her house.

TIÁN

sweet;
pleasant

舌 shows the tongue (千) in the mouth (口). 甘 depicts something (一) worth holding in the mouth (口). So 甜 means sweet (甘) to the tongue (舌). However, beware of anything sweet from the tongue, for the tongue is like a sharp knife that kills without drawing blood. Hence the proverb: "Bitter words are medicine; sweet words bring illness."

ノ ニ 千 千 舌 舌 舌 甜 甜 甜 甜

甜美	tián měi	sweet; luscious; pleasant; refreshing
甜蜜	tiái mì	sweet; happy
甜品	tiái pǐn	sweetmeats
甜头	tián tou	sweet taste; pleasant flavour; good benefit (as an inducement)
甜味	tián wèi	sweet taste
甜言蜜语	tián yán mì yǔ	sweet words and honeyed phrases; fine-sounding words

Example:

这 西 瓜 好 甜 哪 !
Zhè xī guā hǎo tián na
This watermelon is really sweet!

103

叫 **JIÀO** call

叫 is to call out (口) the measure (斗). The ancient form of 斗 depicts a measuring ladle ( ) with ten (十): . Although vendors shout out their wares, a melon seller never cries "Bitter melons!" nor a wine seller "Thin wine!"

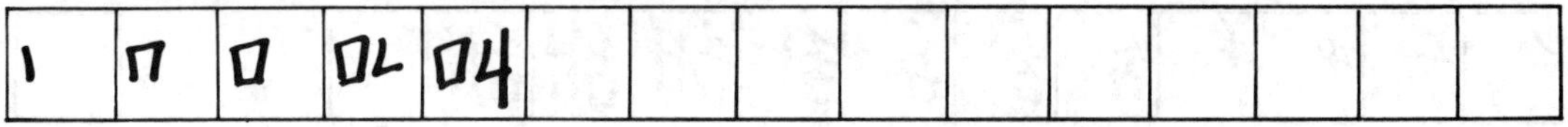

叫喊	jiào hǎn	shout; yell; howl
叫好	jiào hǎo	applaud
叫唤	jiào huan	cry out; call out
叫苦	jiào kǔ	complain of hardship or suffering; moan and groan
叫骂	jiào mà	shout curses
叫门	jiào mén	call at the door to be let in
叫醒	jiào xǐng	wake up; awaken
叫座	jiào zuò	draw a large audience; draw well; appeal to the audience

Example:

外 边 有 人 叫 你 。

Wài bian yǒu rén jiào nǐ

Somebody outside is calling you.

听 （聽）

TĪNG   hear; listen

聽 is the rectification (直 or 㥁) of the heart (心) of a listener or disciple (壬) by his ear (耳); hence to listen or obey. The simplified form 听 combines 口 (mouth) with 斤 (discerning), i.e., to discern what comes from the mouth — by listening. It may even suggest that most people today listen with their mouths!

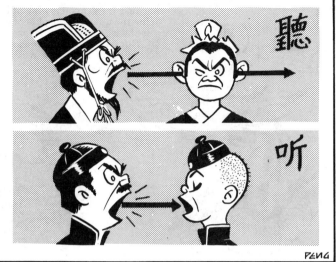

| 一 | 丨 | 口 | 口′ | 叮 | 听 | 听 | | | | | | | |

听从	tīng cóng	obey; heed; comply with
听而不闻	tīng ér bù wén	hear but pay no attention
听话	tīng huà	be obedient
听觉	tīng jué	sense of hearing
听说	tīng shuō	be told; hear of
听筒	tīng tǒng	(telephone) receiver; headphone; earphone
听写	tīng xiě	dictation
听众	tīng zhòng	audience; listeners

Example:

我 们 从 来 没 听 说 过 这 种 事 。
Wǒ men cóng lái méi tīng shuō guō zhè zhǒng shì

We've never heard of such a thing.

聋（聾）

LÓNG deaf

Because the dragon is king of the supernatural creatures (the others being the unicorn, the phoenix and the tortoise), it can afford to turn a deaf ear to anything. Hence dragon's (龙) ear (耳), meaning deaf: 聋. But let not those who cannot hear well lose heart: "In the kingdom of the deaf, the one-eared man is king!"

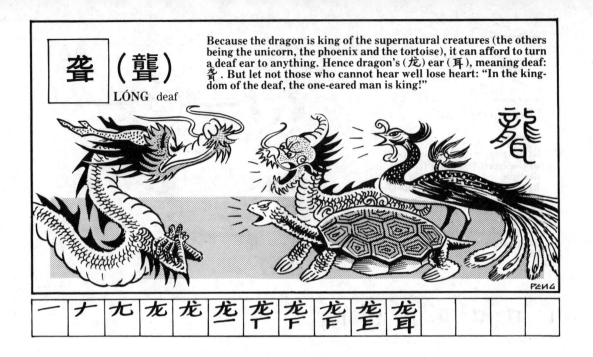

| 一 | 十 | 尤 | 龙 | 龙 | 龙 | 龙 | 龙 | 龙 | 聋 | 聋 | | |

| 聋哑 | lóng yǎ | deaf and dumb; deaf-mute |
| 聋子 | lóng zi | a deaf person |

Example:

她 在 一 间 聋 哑 学 校 当 教 员 。

Tā zài yì jiān lóng yǎ xué xiào dāng jiào yuán

She works as a teacher in the school for deaf-mutes.

喜

xǐ

happiness; pleasure

喜 or happiness is expressed by 壴 (music) and 口 (singing). 壴 depicts the ancient drum on its stand (豆) with its stretched skin (一) and a straightened right hand (屮) striking it. 口 represents the mouth singing. True happiness, however, comes from unselfish giving; and when you make two people happy, one of them is probably you.

| 一 | 十 | 士 | 吉 | 吉 | 吉 | 壴 | 喜 | 喜 | 喜 | 喜 | 喜 |

喜爱	xǐ ài	like; love; be fond of; be keen on
喜欢	xǐ huan	like; love; happy; elated; filled with joy
喜酒	xǐ jiǔ	wedding feast
喜剧	xǐ jù	comedy
喜怒无常	xǐ nù wú cháng	subject to changing moods
喜气洋洋	xǐ qì yáng yáng	full of joy; jubilant
喜事	xǐ shì	happy event; wedding
喜新厌旧	xǐ xīn yàn jiù	love the new and loathe the old — be fickle in affection

Example:

这 孩 子 真 讨 人 喜 欢 。
Zhè hái zi zhēn tǎo rén xǐ huan

This is a lovable child.

春

CHŪN

spring

, the seal character for spring (春), signifies the growth and outburst (屯) of vegetation (屮屮) under the influence of the sun (⊖). As unpredictable and changeable as the weather, spring comes either early or late each year. Hence the proverb: "Spring has a stepmother's face."

一 二 三 尹 夫 夬 春 春 春

春风满面	chūn fēng mǎn miàn	beaming with satisfaction; radiant with happiness
春光	chūn guāng	sights and sounds of spring
春季	chūn jì	spring; springtime
春卷	chūn juǎn	spring roll
春联	chūn lián	Spring Festival couplets (pasted on gateposts or door panels); New Year scrolls
春秋	chūn qiū	spring and autumn; year; the Spring and Autumn Period (770-476 B.C.)
春天	chūn tiān	spring; springtime

Example:

看 他 春 风 满 面， 一 定 有 好 消 息 告 诉 我 们 。
Kàn tā chūn fēng mǎn miàn yí dìng yǒu hǎo xiāo xi gào su wǒ men

His face is beaming with happiness; he must have some good news for us.

108

唱

CHÀNG sing

昌 is composed of 日 (sun) and 曰 (speak). 曰 is the mouth (口) that exhales a breath; by extension, exhalation and emanation. So 昌 means prosperous or splendid, just as the sun sends forth rays and the mouth puts forth words.

唱 therefore refers to singing which produces a more refined quality of the voice than an ordinary conversation.

唱词	chàng cí	libretto; words of a ballad
唱歌	chàng gē	sing (a song)
唱工	chàng gōng	art of singing; singing
唱片	chàng piàn	gramophone record
唱诗班	chàng shī bān	choir
电唱机	diàn chàng jī	record player

Example:

她 很 会 唱 歌 。
Tā hěn huì chàng gē
She is a good singer.

GĒ

song

可 is an exclamation of approval (丁) from the mouth (口) and means can or may.
哥 is 可 doubled, suggesting singing, now used for addressing elder brother by sound loan.
歌 adds breath (欠) to singing (哥) to produce a song.

一 丁 一 可 可 可 哥 哥 哥 哥 哥 歌 歌 歌

歌本	gē běn	songbook
歌词	gē cí	words of a song
歌功颂德	gē gōng sòng dé	eulogize somebody's virtues and achievements
歌喉	gē hóu	(singer's) voice
歌剧	gē jù	opera
歌谱	gē pǔ	music of a song

歌曲	gē qǔ	song
歌手	gē shǒu	singer; vocalist
歌颂	gē sòng	sing the praises of
歌舞	gē wǔ	song and dance
歌谣	gē yáo	ballad; folk song; nursery rhyme
歌咏比赛	gē yǒng bǐ sài	singing contest

Example:

这 首 歌 的 歌 词 很 动 人 。
Zhè shǒu gē de gē cí hěn dòng rén
The words of this song are most touching.

鸣 （鳴）

MÍNG cry of bird,
    animal or insect

Because a bird (鸟) chirps
or sings with its mouth (口),
we have the character 鸣
applied to the cry of birds,
animals or insects. Some-
times even man crows — like
the rooster that thinks the
sun rises to hear him crow.

丶 冂 口 口' 叮 叮 鸣 鸣

鸡鸣	jī míng	the crow of a cock
鸣谢	míng xiè	express one's thanks formally
鸣放	míng fàng	airing of views
鸣锣开道	míng luó kāi dào	beat gongs to clear the way (for officials in feudal times);
		prepare the public for a coming event
鸣禽	míng qín	songbird; singing bird
鸣冤叫屈	míng yuān jiào qū	complain and call for redress; voice grievances

Example:

钟 鸣 三 下 。
Zhōng míng sān xià
The clock struck three.

111

吐　TǓ　spit out
　　TÙ　vomit

The ideograph 吐, literally from mouth (口) to earth (土), means to spit or vomit. Figuratively, it means to disclose or reveal the truth — like spilling the beans or letting the cat out of the bag. In this sense, beware: "A very big secret can be vomited out of a little mouth."

| 丨 | 冂 | 口 | 口一 | 口十 | 吐 | | | | | | | | |

吐露	tǔ lù	reveal; tell
吐气	tǔ qì	feel elated after unburdening oneself of resentment
吐沫	tù mo	saliva; spittle; spit
吐血	tù xiě	spitting blood; haematemesis
吐泻	tù xiè	vomitting and diarrhoea

Example:

他 不 愿 意 吐 露 真 情 。
Tā　bú　yuàn　yì　tǔ　lù　zhēn　qíng

He was reluctant to reveal the truth.

112

如

RÚ

like; as

Ideographically, 如 is to speak (口) like or as a woman (女), that is, appropriately to the circumstances and the disposition of the man she desires to influence. Testifying to such persuasive, womanly skill is the saying: "The walls of a city are raised by men's wisdom but overthrown by women's wiles."

人	女	女	如	如	如								

如常　　　rú cháng　　as usual
如此　　　rú cǐ　　　so; such; in this way
如此而已　rú cǐ ér yǐ　that's what it all adds up to
如果　　　rú guǒ　　if; in case; in the event of
如何　　　rú hé　　　how; what
如今　　　rú jīn　　　nowadays; now
如期　　　rú qī　　　as scheduled; on schedule

如意　　　rú yì　　　as one wishes
如意算盘　rú yì suàn pan　wishful thinking
如鱼得水　rú yú dé shuǐ　feel just like fish in water; be in one's element
如愿以偿　rú yuàn yǐ cháng　have one's wish fulfilled; achieve what one wishes

Example:

会　议　将　如　期　召　开　。
Huì　yì　jiāng　rú　qī　zhào　kāi

The conference will be convened as scheduled.

娘 NÍANG

mother;
young mother

The modern form 娘 signifies a woman (女) who is virtuous and respectable (良) — a good woman, a mother or a young woman.

The old form 孃 stands for a homely and helpful (襄) woman (女). Of such a woman it is said: "The homely woman is precious in the home, but at a feast the beautiful one is preferred."

PENG

く　女　女　女ˊ　女ㄱ　女ㅋ　女ㅌ　娘　娘　娘

新娘	xīn niáng	bride
娘家	niáng jia	a married woman's parents' home
娘娘	niáng niang	empress or imperial concubine of the first rank; goddess
娘胎	niǎng tāi	mother's womb

Example:

嫂 嫂 回 娘 家 去 了 。

Sǎo sao huí niáng jia qù le

My sister-in-low has gone to visit her parents.

114

妙 MIÀO wonderful

At 17 or 18 there are no ugly girls. So the characters 少 (young) and 女 (woman) together form the ideograph 妙, an adjective of admiration meaning wonderful, excellent and beautiful. Notwithstanding this, "Ugly wives and stupid servant girls are treasures above price."

妙不可言	miào bù kě yán	too wonderful for words; most intriguing
妙计	miào jì	excellent plan; brilliant scheme
妙诀	miào jué	a clever way of doing something; knack
妙趣横生	miào qù héng shēng	full of wit and humour; very witty
妙手回春	miào shǒu huí chūn	(of a doctor) effect a miraculous cure and bring the dying back to life
妙用	miào yòng	magical effect
妙语	miào yǔ	witty remark; witticism

Example:

他 回 答 得 很 妙 。
Tā huí dá dé hěn miào

He made a clever answer.

KÈ

guest;
visitor

夊 represents a man following his own way.
各 signifies his going his way (夊) without heeding advice (口); by extension, each or every.
客 is a guest — one who has his way under another's roof (宀). No wonder "the host is happy when the guest is gone."

`、` `ハ` `宀` `宀` `夕` `宓` `宓` `客` `客`

客船	kè chuán	passenger ship	
客串	kè chuàn	be a guest performer	
客队	kè duì	(sports) visiting team	
客房	kè fáng	guest room	
客观	kè guān	objective	
客机	kè jī	passenger plane; airliner	

客满	kè mǎn	(of theatre tickets, etc.) sold out; full house
客气	kè qi	polite; courteous; dest
客人	kè rén	visitor; guest
客套	kè tào	polite formula; civilities

Example:

他 对 人 很 客 气 。

Tā duì rén hěn kè qi

He is very polite to people.

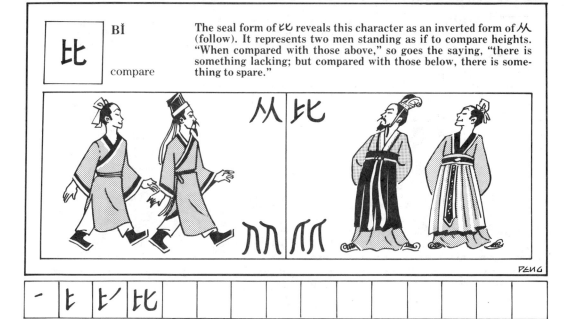

| 比 | **BǏ** compare | The seal form of 比 reveals this character as an inverted form of 从 (follow). It represents two men standing as if to compare heights. "When compared with those above," so goes the saying, "there is something lacking; but compared with those below, there is something to spare." |

| 一 | 七 | 七ʼ | 比 | | | | | | | | | | | | | |

比方	bǐ fang	analogy; instance
比分	bǐ fēn	score
比价	bǐ jià	price relations; parity; rate of exchange
比较	bǐ jiào	compare; contrast; fairly; comparatively; quite; rather
比率	bǐ lǜ	ratio; rate
比如	bǐ rú	for example; for instance
比赛	bǐ sài	match; competition
比喻	bǐ yù	metaphor; analogy

Example:

这 只 是 一 个 比 喻 的 说 法 。
Zhè zhǐ shì yī ge bǐ yù de shuō fa

This is just a figure of speech.

117

BEI
back; oppose

BĒI
carry on the back

A person sitting facing the south (as is the custom) and back to back with another suggests north: 北. Turning one's back on another signifies opposition. Hence 背, referring to the back (北) of the body (月), may mean to oppose or to carry on the back.

PENG

| 一 | 一 | ㇐ | 北 | 北 | 北 | 背 | 背 | 背 | | | | |

背痛	bèi tòng	backache
背地里	bèi dì li	behind somebody's back; privately; on the sly
背后	bèi hòu	behind; at the back; in the rear
背脊	bèi jǐ	the back of the human body
背井离乡	bèi jǐng lí xiāng	leave one's native place (especially against one's will)
背景	bèi jǐng	background; backdrop
背叛	bèi pàn	betray; forsake
背诵	bèi sòng	recite; repeat from memory

Example:

我 怕 背 不 起 这 样 的 责 任 。
Wǒ pà bēi bù qǐ zhè yàng de zé rèn
I'm afraid I can't shoulder such a responsibility

118

凶

XĪONG

unfortunate; ominous

凶 means unfortunate, symbolized by a man falling upside down (ㄨ) into a pit (凵). Calamities do not always come by accident. According to the proverb, "Calamity comes by means of the mouth."

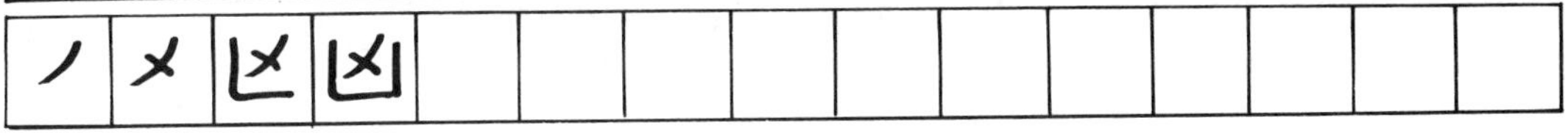

凶残	xiōng cán	fierce and cruel; savage and cruel
凶多吉少	xiōng duō jí shǎo	bode ill rather than well; be fraught with grim possibilities
凶恶	xiōng è	fierce, ferocious; fiendish
凶犯	xiōng fàn	one who has committed homicide; murderer
凶猛	xiōng měng	violent; ferocious
凶器	xiōng qì	tool or weapon for criminal purposes; lethal weapon
凶杀	xiōng shā	homicide; murder
凶手	xiōng shǒu	murderer; assassin; assailant

Example:

这 个 人 样 子 真 凶 。

Zhè ge rén yàng zi zhēn xiōng

This chap looks really fierce.

答

DÁ   reply; answer

Because of its beauty, design and harmony (合), the bamboo (竹) is used here as a perfect example of an answer or reply: 答. However, like bamboos, answers come in various lengths. Many a short question is evaded by a long answer.

丿　𠂉　𠂉　𠂊　竹　𥫗　𥫗　笅　笘　答　答

答非所问	dá fēi suǒ wèn	an irrelevent answer
答案	dá àn	answer; solution; key
答辩	dá biàn	reply (to a charge, query or an argument)
答词	dá cí	thank-you speech; answering speech; reply
答复	dá fù	answer; reply
答谢	dá xiè	express appreciation; acknowledge
答应	dá ying	answer; respond; agree; promise; comply with

Example:

你 怎 么 不 答 话 ？
Nǐ zěn me bù dá huà

Why don't you answer?

篮 （籃）

LÁN   basket

籃 is to bend over (臥) a full vase (皿) to examine its contents; by extension, to oversee those who are confined in a prison. When the bamboo radical 竹 is added, we have a bamboo container to confine goods for safe transportation —a basket: 籃, now simplified to 篮.

ノ	𠂉	𠂆丨	𠂆ノ	𥫗	𥫗	竹	笁	笁	笁	笁	箳	篮	篮	篮

投篮	tóu lán	(basketball) shoot a basket
篮球	lán qiú	basketball
篮圈	lán quān	(basketball) ring; hoop
篮子	lán zi	basket

Example:

今 天 学 校 举 行 了 一 场 篮 球 比 赛 。
Jīn tiān xué xiào jǔ xíng le yī chǎng lán qiú bǐ sài
A basketball match was held in the school today.

121

井 JǏNG well

Originally the seal form 丼 represented fields divided among eight families, with the well in the middle plot to serve the public. The well also serves to expose man's inclination to faultfinding: "One does not blame the shortness of the rope, but the deepness of the well."

一 二 非 井

矿井	kuàng jǐng	pit; mine
油井	yóu jǐng	oil well; neat; orderly
井场	jǐng cháng	well site
井底之蛙	jǐng dǐ zhī wā	a frog in a well — a person with a very limited outlook
井架	jǐng jià	derrick
井井有条	jǐng jǐng yǒu tiáo	in perfect order; shipshape; methodical
井水不犯河水	jǐng shuǐ bú fàn hé shuǐ	well water does not intrude into river water — I'll mind my own business, you mind yours

Example:

各 种 仪 器 、 工 具 摆 得 井 井 有 条 。

Gè zhǒng yí qì   gōng jù bǎi de jǐng jǐng yǒu tiáo

All the instruments and tools are kept in perfect order.

122

SHÍ

stone

石 is a picture of a piece of stone or rock (口) falling from a cliff (厂).

岩 is a steep rock (石) or cliff that looks like a hill (山). The rock, being strong, symbolizes integrity. Hence: "Slander cannot destroy an honest man; when the flood recedes the rock appears."

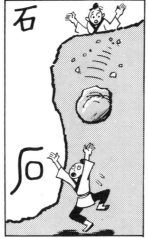

一 丁 丆 石 石

石斑鱼	shí bān yú	grouper
石壁	shí bì	cliff; precipice
石沉大海	shí chén dà hǎi	like a stone dropped into the sea — disappear forever
石雕	shí diāo	stone carving; carved stone
石膏	shí gāo	gypsum; plaster stone
石工	shígōng	masonry; stonemason; mason

石灰	shí huī	lime
石榴	shí liu	pomegranate
石头	shí tou	stone; rock
石印	shí yìn	lithographic printing; lithography
石英	shí yīng	quartz
石油	shí yóu	petroleum; oil
石子	shí zǐ	cobblestone; cobble; pebble

Example:

这 块 石 头 是 从 山 上 拾 回 来 的 。

Zhè kuài shí tou shì cóng shān shàng shí huí lai de

This stone was picked up from the mountain.

仙	XĪAN fairy; recluse

The ancient form 僊 signifies a human (儿) who rises by climbing with his head (囟) and four hands (𦥑), probably after the manner of a monkey. An official seal (㔾) is added to denote promotion. The modern form 仙 associates person (亻) with mountain (山), suggesting recluse and fairy.

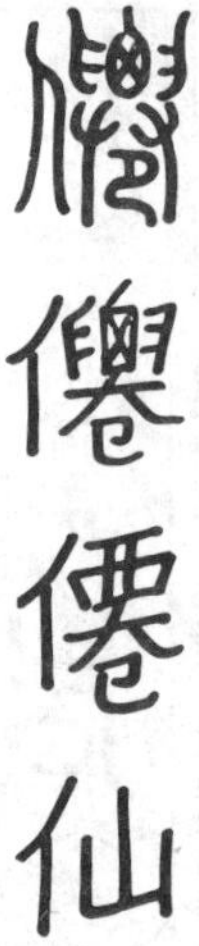

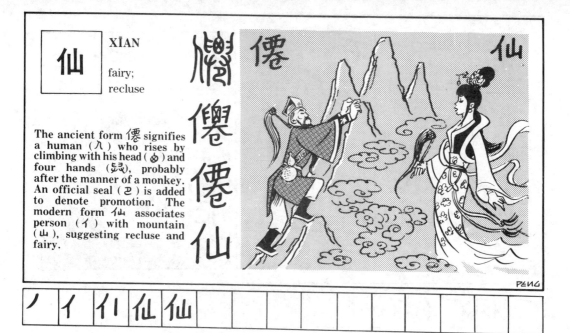

ノ	亻	亻丨	仙	仙										

仙丹	xiān dān	elixir of life
仙姑	xiāng gū	female immortal; sorceress
仙鹤	xiān hè	red-crowned crane
仙境	xiān jìng	fairyland; wonderland; paradise
仙女	xiān nǚ	female celestial; fairy maiden
仙人掌	xiān rén zhǎng	cactus

Example:

这 棵 仙 人 掌 有 很 多 刺 。
Zhè kē xiān rén zhǎng yǒu hěn duō cì
This cactus is covered with prickles.

GĀO

高

high; tall

高 is a pictograph of a high tower or pavilion (古) on a lofty sub-structure (冂) equipped with a hall (口). It stands for high. When it comes to position, no person stoops so low as the one most eager to rise high in the world. But beware: "He who climbs too high will have a heavy fall."

丶 亠 亠 六 亩 亠 高 高 高 高

高傲	gāo ào	supercilious; arrogant	
高超音速	gāo chāo yīn sù	hypersonic speed	
高潮	gāo cháo	high tide; upsurge; climax	
高大	gāo dà	tall and big; tall	
高度	gāo dù	altitude; height	
高峰	gāo fēng	peak; summit; height	
高贵	gāo guì	noble; high; elitist	

高级	gāo jí	senior; high-ranking
高见	gāo jiàn	your brilliant idea
高举	gāo jǔ	hold high; hold aloft
高烧	gāo shāo	high fever
高兴	gāo xìng	glad; happy; cheerful
高血压	gāo xuè yā	hypertension
高原	gāo yuán	plateau; highland

Example:

你 不 高 兴 去 就 甭 去 了 。
Nǐ bù gāo xìng qù jiù béng qù le
You needn't go if you don't feel like it.

125

JĪNG

京

capital city

京 is derived from 高 (high). It is a contraction of 高 with the lower part replaced by 小, a pivot, conveying the idea of loftiness and centrality. So lofty is the capital city that it is said: "One who can speak, speaks of the city; one who cannot, talks merely of household affairs."

`丶  一  亠  古  古  亨  京  京`

| 京城 | jīng chéng | the capital of a country |
| 京剧 | jīng jù | Beijing opera |

Example:

妈 妈 最 喜 欢 看 京 剧 。
Mā ma zuì xǐ huan kàn jīng jù
My mother especially likes to watch Beijing opera.

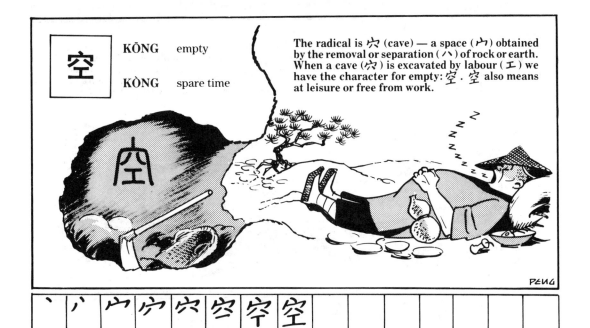

空　KŌNG　empty

空　KÒNG　spare time

The radical is 穴 (cave) — a space (宀) obtained by the removal or separation (八) of rock or earth. When a cave (穴) is excavated by labour (工) we have the character for empty: 空. 空 also means at leisure or free from work.

丶　丷　宀　宀　穴　空　空　空

空洞	kōng dòng	cavity; empty	空阔	kōng kuò	open; spacious
空防	kōng fáng	air defence	空前绝后	kōng qián jué hòu	unprecedented
空话	kōng huà	empty talk; idle talk	空头支票	kōng tóu zhī piào	dud cheque
空欢喜	kōng huān xi	rejoice too soon	空想	kōng xiǎng	idle dream; fantasy
空间	kōng jiān	space	空运	kōng yùn	air transport; airlift
空军	kōng jūn	air force	空中	kōng zhōng	in the sky; aerial; overhead

Example:

别 空 想 了 ， 还 是 从 实 际 出 发 吧 。

Bié kōng xiǎng le hái shì cóng shí jì chū fā ba

Stop daydreaming. Be realistic.

船 **CHUÁN**

boat; ship

As a memory aid, 船 could refer to a boat (舟) with eight (八) survivors or mouths (口) — an allusion to Noah's Ark. The radical 舟 is a picture of a boat. The phonetic 㕣 probably means a coast; so 船 is a coastal (沿) vessel (舟). No matter how useful such a vessel is, "Like a thread without a needle, a boat is useless without water."

丿 丨 几 丹 舟 舟 舟 舟 舟 船 船

船埠	chuán bù	wharf; quay
船壳	chuán ké	hull
船尾	chuán wěi	stern
船坞	chuán wù	dock; shipyard
船员	chuán yuán	(ship's) crew
船长	chuán zhǎng	captain; skipper
船只	chuán zhǐ	shipping; vessels

Example:

这 艘 船 的 船 员 们 都 很 勤 劳 。
Zhè sōu chuán de chuán yuán men dōu hěn qín láo
The sailors on this ship are hardworking.

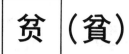

PÍN poor

The radical 貝 , a picture of cowrie shells once used as money, represents wealth. 分 is to divide or scatter. So 貧 is to squander (分) one's wealth (貝) — to be poor. Even the poor cannot afford to ignore the warning: "If the poor associates with the rich, he will soon have no trousers to wear."

| 丿 | 八 | 分 | 分 | 分 | 貧 | 贫 | 贫 | | | | | |

贫病交迫	pín bìng jiāo pò	suffering from both poverty and sickness
贫乏	pín fá	poor; short; lacking
贫寒	pín hán	poor; poverty-stricken
贫困	pín kùn	poor; impoverished; in straitened circumstances
贫民	pín mín	poor people; pauper
贫穷	pín qióng	poor; needy; impoverished
贫血	pín xuè	anaemia

Example:

在 他 贫 病 交 迫 的 时 候 ， 大 家 都 帮 助 他 。
Zài tā pín bìng jiāo pò de shí hou   dà jiā dōu bāng zhù tā
Everybody helped him out when he was sick and in poverty.

129

圆 （圓）

YUÁN   round; dollar

This character for round or dollar has undergone many changes since its original form: ○. The ideograph 員, meaning round (○) like a cowrie (貝), soon replaced it. Then it was altered to 圓, being reclarified and surrounded by 囗. Although hollowed out to 圆, the dollar is still changeable; it's easier to change dollars into goods than goods into dollars!

| 丨 | 冂 | 冂 | 冂 | 冂 | 冃 | 冄 | 冋 | 圆 | 圆 | | | |

圆规	yuán guī	compasses	
圆滑	yuán huá	smooth and evasive; slick and sly	
圆满	yuán mǎn	satisfactory	
圆圈	yuán quān	circle; ring	
圆舞曲	yuán wǔ qǔ	waltz	
圆形	yuán xíng	circular; round	
圆周	yuán zhōu	circumference	
圆珠笔	yuán zhū bǐ	ball-point pen; ball-pen	

Example:

问 题 圆 满 地 解 决 了 。
Wèn tí yuán mǎn de jiě jué le

The problem has been solved satisfactorily.

儿 （兒）

ÉR infant; child

儿 is a pictograph of the growing child — from the crawling infant with open fontanels (𡕾) to the little toddler (兒) with wobbly legs, now simplified to its present form: 儿 . The loving care shown in the delineation of this character calls to mind the saying: "To understand your parents' love, raise your own children."

ノ	儿											

儿歌	ér gē	children's song; nursery rhymes
儿科	ér kē	(department of) paediatrics
儿女	ér nǚ	sons and daughters; children
儿孙	ér sūn	children and grandchildren; descendants
儿童	ér tóng	children

Example:

他　有　一　儿　一　女　。
Tā　yǒu　yī　ér　yī　nǚ

He has a son and a daughter.

131

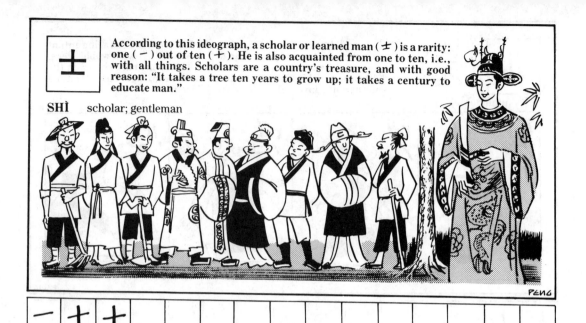

According to this ideograph, a scholar or learned man (士) is a rarity: one (一) out of ten (十). He is also acquainted from one to ten, i.e., with all things. Scholars are a country's treasure, and with good reason: "It takes a tree ten years to grow up; it takes a century to educate man."

SHÌ   scholar; gentleman

一	十	士									

士兵	shì bīng	rank-and-file soldiers; privates
士女	shì nǚ	young men and women
士气	shì qì	morale
士绅	shì shēn	gentry
士卒	shì zú	soldiers; privates

Example:

我 军 士 气 高 昂 。
Wǒ jūn shì qì gāo áng
Our army's morale is high.

	ZUÒ	做 sets forth man (亻) with a cause (故) to produce an effect. Hence the meaning: to make or produce. It also suggests man (亻) toiling (夊) until he gets old (古), sometimes for a fruitless cause. In the words of the proverb: "The hard work of a hundred years may be destroyed in an hour."
做	make; produce	

PENG

ノ 亻 仁 什 什 估 估 估′ 估ˊ 做ˊ 做

做东	zuò dōng	play the host
做法	zuò fǎ	way of doing or making a thing
做工	zuò gōng	do manual work; work
做鬼	zuò guǐ	play tricks; play an underhand game
做客	zuò kè	be a guest
做礼拜	zuò lǐ bài	go to church; be at church
做梦	zuò mèng	have a dream; dream
做贼心虚	zuò zéi xīn xū	have a guilty conscience

Example:

我 昨 天 到 一 个 老 朋 友 家 里 去 做 客 。
Wǒ zuó tiān dào yī ge lǎo péng you jiā lǐ qù zuò kè
I was a guest at an old friend's yesterday.

133

众 （衆）

ZHÒNG   crowd; many

The seal form 众 shows three or many persons (从从) as viewed by the eye (⊙). Modified to 眾, it was again altered to 众 — three persons, representing a crowd. It's easier to follow the crowd than to get the crowd to follow you. In the words of the proverb: "An army of a 1000 is easy to find; but, ah, how difficult to find a general!"

PENG

丿	人	今	众	分	众					

众多	zhòng duō	multitudinous; numerous
众口难调	zhòng kǒu nán tiáo	it is difficult to cater for all tastes
众口一词	zhòng kǒu yī cí	with one voice; unanimously
众目睽睽	zhòng mù kuí kuí	the eyes of the masses are fixed on somebody or something
众人	zhòng rén	everybody
众望	zhòng wàng	people's expectations

Example:

他 不 负 众 望 ， 得 到 冠 军 。
Tā bú fù zhòng wàng   dé dào guàn jūn

He had come up to the people's expectations when he won the championship.

价 (價)

JÌA   price; value

The ideograph for price (價) is derived by putting 亻, man, the buyer against 賈, the seller. 賈, the seller, marks up the price to cover (西) his goods with value in cowries (貝). Paradoxically, the highest price you can pay for anything is to get it for nothing.

丿 亻 亻 价 价 价

估价	gū jià	estimate the value of; evaluate
讲价	jiǎng jià	bargain
价格	jià gé	price
价目	jià mù	marked price
价值	jià zhí	value; worth
价值连城	jià zhí lián chéng	worth several cities — invaluable; priceless

Example:

这 些 资 料 对 我 们 很 有 价 值 。
Zhè xiē zī liào duì wǒ men hěn yǒu jià zhí
This data is of great value to us

135

话（話）

HUÀ speech; words

話, meaning words or speech, is signified by words (言) of the tongue (舌).
講, meaning to speak or explain, is suggested by words (言) set in order (冓), 冓 being a graphic representation of the framework of a building. 講 is simplified to 讲. Sense is often linked with speech: "The full teapot makes no sound; the half-empty teapot makes much noise."

丶　讠　讠　讠　讠　话　话

话别	huà bié	say a few parting words; say good-bye
话柄	huà bǐng	subject for ridicule
话旧	huà jiù	talk over old times; reminisce
话剧	huà jù	modern drama; stage play
话里有话	huà lǐ yǒu huà	the words mean more than they say
话题	huà tí	subject of a talk; topic of conversation
话筒	huà tǒng	microphone; telephone transmitter; megaphone
话头	huà tóu	thread of discourse

Example:

她　喜　欢　看　我　演　的　话　剧　。
Tā　xǔ　huan　kàn　wǒ　yǎn　de　huà　jù

She likes the plays that I perform in.

语 (語)

YǓ language

吾, or five (五) mouths (口), stands for we, I, our or my. So our or my (吾) words (言) become language (語). Language is used in many ways. Some people use it to express thought, some to conceal thought, but most use it to replace thought.

` 讠 讠 讠 语 语 语 语 语

甜言蜜语	tián yán mì yǔ	honeyed words	语录	yǔ lù	recorded utterance; quotation
语词	yǔ cí	words and phrases	语气	yǔ qì	tone; manner of speaking
语调	yǔ diào	intonation	语无伦次	yǔ wú lún cì	speak incoherently
语法	yǔ fǎ	grammar	语言	yǔ yán	language
语汇	yǔ huì	vocabulary	语音	yǔ yīn	speech sounds; pronunciation
语句	yǔ jù	sentence			

Example:

她 的 语 音 好 。

Tā de yǔ yīn hǎo

She has good pronunciation.

去 QÙ

go; leave

去 is a pictograph of an empty vessel (厶) and its cover (土). The meaning "go" comes from the removal of the cover and contents of the vessel.
来 , meaning "come", is a pictograph of growing wheat or barley, gratefully acknowledged as having come from the heavens above.

一 十 土 去 去

去处	qù chù	place to go; whereabouts
去粗取精	qù cū qǔ jīng	discard the dross and select the essential
去垢剂	qù gòu jì	detergent
去路	qù lù	the way along which one is going; outlet
去年	qù nián	last year
去世	qù shì	(of grown-up people) die; pass away
去污粉	qù wū fěn	household cleanser; cleanser
去向	qù xiàng	the direction in which somebody or something has gone

Example:

有 谁 知 道 他 的 去 处 ?
Yǒu shuí zhī dao tā de qù chù
Who knows his where abouts?

HUÍ return

回 represents an eddy, like the curling clouds of smoke or whirlpools in water; or probably an object that rolls or turns on an axis; hence the idea of revolving or returning.

回避	huí bì	evade; dodge	
回驳	huí bó	refute	
回肠荡气	huí cháng dàng qì	(of music, poems, etc.) soulstirring; heartrending	
回程	huí chéng	return trip	
回答	huí dá	answer; reply; response	
回顾	huí gù	look back; review	

回击	huí jī	return fire; counterattack
回教	Huí jiào	Islam
回绝	huí jué	decline, refuse
回来	huí lai	return; be back
回头	huí tóu	turn round; repent; later
回想	huí xiǎng	think back; recollect

Example:

他 马 上 就 回 来 。

Tā mǎ shàng jiù huí lai

He'll be back in a minute.

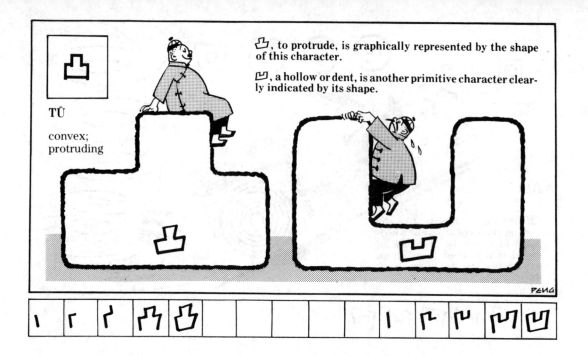

TŪ

convex;
protruding

凸, to protrude, is graphically represented by the shape of this character.

凹, a hollow or dent, is another primitive character clearly indicated by its shape.

凸版印刷	tū bǎn yìn shuā	letterpress; relief or typographic printing
凸窗	tū chuāng	bay window
凸轮	tū lún	cam
凸面镜	tū miàn jìng	convex mirror
凸透镜	tū tòu jìng	convex lens

凹版印刷	āo bǎn yìn shuā	intaglio or gravure printing
凹面镜	āo miàn jìng	concave mirror
凹透镜	āo tòu jìng	concave lens
凹凸印刷	āo tū yìn shuā	embossing; die stamping
凹陷	āo xiàn	hollow; depressed

Example:

这 条 路 凹 凸 不 平 。
Zhè tiáo lù āo tū bù píng

This road is full of bumps and holes.

140

INDEX　附录

ài	爱	1:171	bù	不	2:100	cuàn	窜	2:84	ēn	恩	2:4
ān	安	1:4		布	3:33				ér	儿	3:131
āo	凹	3:140		步	1:77	dá	答	3:120	ěr	耳	1:58
						dà	大	1:14			
						dài	带	3:37	fǎ	法	3:83
bā	八	1:62	cài	菜	3:102		待	3:70	fà	发	3:95
bà	爸	3:54	cǎo	草	1:131	dàn	旦	1:29	fán	烦	3:76
bái	白	1:28	chá	茶	1:135		蛋	2:30	fàn	犯	2:60
bài	拜	3:99	cháng	常	3:39	dāo	刀	2:35		饭	3:16
bàn	办	3:73	chàng	唱	3:109	dǎo	岛	1:105	fāng	方	2:16
	半	1:154	cháo	巢	1:166	dào	道	3:91	fáng	房	2:17
	伴	1:155	chē	车	3:21	dé	得	3:63	fàng	放	3:100
bāng	帮	3:40	chén	尘	2:72		德	3:64	fēi	飞	1:107
bǎo	宝	2:31	chǐ	齿	1:73	dì	帝	3:36	fèi	吠	2:51
	饱	3:17	chóng	虫	2:124	diǎn	点	1:130		费	2:41
bèi	贝	1:86	chóu	愁	1:143	diàn	电	1:99	fēn	分	2:36
	背	3:118	chǒu	丑	2:48	diē	爹	3:54	fěn	粉	3:12
	被	3:43	chòu	臭	2:53	dié	蝶	2:127	fēng	风	2:131
běn	本	1:162	chū	出	1:83	dīng	钉	2:14		蜂	2:126
bǐ	比	3:117	chuān	川	1:102	dìng	定	2:33	fèng	凤	2:98
	笔	1:138	chuán	船	3:128	dōng	东	1:34	fū	夫	1:16
biǎo	表	3:44	chuáng	床	3:46	duì	兑	1:63	fú	弗	2:40
bié	别	2:38	chuǎng	闯	2:70	duō	多	3:52		伏	2:55
bīng	兵	2:21	chūn	春	3:108				fù	父	3:31
bīng	冰	1:93	cōng	匆	1:176					妇	3:35
bìng	病	3:88		聪	2:1	è or wù	恶	2:3		富	2:30
bō	波	3:80	cóng	从	3:61	è	饿	3:18			

gān	甘	1:149		合	2:5	jiān	尖	1:21	kāi	开	2:29
gāo	羔	1:116		和	1:147		监	3:121	kàn	看	1:49
	高	3:125	hēi	黑	1:128	jiàn	见	1:48	kě	渴	3:82
gào	告	1:156	hěn	狠	2:61		件	1:152	kè	客	3:116
gē	戈	1:42		很	3:66		贱	1:87		课	1:165
	歌	3:110	hōng	轰	3:22	jiāng	将	3:48	kōng	空	3:127
	鸽	2:97	hóng	红	2:136	jiǎng	讲	3:136	kǒu	口	1:50
geǐ	给	2:137	hóu	猴	2:50	jiàng	匠	2:20	kū	枯	3:85
gōng	工	1:53	hòu	后	3:69	jiāo	焦	2:91		哭	2:54
	弓	2:39	hǔ	虎	2:75	jiǎo	角	2:109	kù	库	3:23
	公	2:132	hù	户	2:15	jiào	叫	3:104		裤	3:42
	功	3:71	huā	花	1:34		骄	3:27	kuài	快	1:175
gǒu	狗	2:49	huà	话	1:57	jiē	街	3:67	kuáng	狂	2:95
gòu	够	3:53		画	2:152	jié	结	2:138			
gǔ	骨	3:119	huī	灰	1:124	jiě	姐	1:170	lái	来	1:161
	古	1:66	huí	回	3:139		解	2:110	lán	篮	3:121
guǎn	馆	3:19	huì	慧	2:2	jīn	巾	3:32	láng	狼	2:62
guāng	光	3:77	huǒ	火	1:121		斤	2:18	láo	牢	1:153
guī	龟	2:105		夥	3:52		今	2:7		劳	3:75
guì	贵	1:88					金	2:10	lǎo	老	2:113
guó	国	3:3	jī	鸡	2:95	jìn	近	2:22	lè	乐	2:146
guǒ	果	1:164	jí	疾	3:90		进	2:89	léi	雷	1:100
				集	2:86	jīng	经	2:142	lí	离	2:94
hǎi	海	3:81	jì	计	1:67		京	3:126	lǐ	李	1:11
hài	害	2:32	jiā	加	3:72		晶	1:30		里	3:5
háng	行	3:62		家	1:7		精	3:13		理	3:6
hǎo			jiǎ	甲	1:31	jǐng	井	3:122	lì	力	1:23
or hào	号	2:76		假	2:121	jiǔ	酒	2:45		立	1:18
hǎo	好	1:3	jià	价	3:135	jūn	军	3:25		丽	2:74
hé	禾	1:141		嫁	1:8					利	2:37

pinyin	char	ref	pinyin	char	ref	pinyin	char	ref	pinyin	char	ref
lián	连	3:29	miàn	面	3:92	pǐ	匹	1:76	sǎn	伞	101
	莲	3:30	miáo	苗	1:132	piàn	片	3:45	sǎo	扫	3:34
liè	劣	3:71	miào	妙	3:115	piào	票	2:114	sēn	森	3:84
lín	林	3:84	míng	名	3:58	pín	贫	3:129	shān	山	1:103
lóng	龙	2:108		明	1:27	pó	婆	3:80		衫	3:42
	聋	3:106		鸣	3:111					煽	1:126
lóu	楼	3:87		铭	3:59	qī	妻	1:9	shàn	扇	1:110
lòu	漏	1:96	mò	末	1:167		栖	1:12	shàng	上	1:36
lǔ	鲁	1:113		墨	1:129	qí	骑	2:66	shāo	烧	1:127
lù	鹿	2:71	mù	木	1:10	qì	气	3:14	shǎo		
lǜ	律	3:68		目	1:47	qiān	金	2:6	or shào	少	1:20
lún	轮	3:24		牧	1:157	qián	钱	2:12	shé	舌	1:56
luó	罗	2:145				qiáng	墙	3:47		蛇	2:129
	骡	2:68	nán	男	3:115	qíng	情	3:98	shēn	身	1:71
luǒ	骆	2:69		难	2:92	qìng	庆	2:73	shēng	生	1:84
			ní	你	1:44	qiū	秋	1:142	shī	师	2:63
mǎ	马	2:65	nián	年	1:148	qǔ	取	1:59		狮	2:63
mǎi	买	1:89	niàn	念	2:8		娶	1:60	shí	十	1:65
mài	卖	1:90	niáng	娘	3:114	qù	去	3:138		石	3:123
máng	盲	3:93	niǎo	鸟	1:104	quán	全	3:9		食	3:15
māo	猫	2:64	niú	牛	1:151		泉	1:94	shǐ	矢	2:43
máo	毛	2:111	nú	奴	1:39		痊	3:10		豕	1:6
mào	帽	3:38	nù	怒	1:69	què	雀	2:85	shì	士	1:132
měi	每	3:81	nǚ	女	1:1	rén	人	1:13		是	1:79
	美	1:117				rì	日	1:25		室	2:104
mèi	妹	1:169	pá	爬	2:115	ròu	肉	1:158		事	2:153
mén	门	2:25	pà	怕	1:70	rú	如	3:113	shǒu	手	1:41
	们	2:26	pàng	胖	1:159	ruǎn	软	3:28	shòu	受	2:118
mèng	梦	3:56	páo	袍	3:43					售	2:90
mǐ	米	3:11	pí	皮	2:120					兽	2:57

shū	书	2:151	tǔ	土	1:81	xiā	虾	2:128	yā	鸭	2:96
shǔ	鼠	2:83		吐	3:112		瞎	3:93	yà	亚	2:3
shuāng	双	2:88	tù	兔	2:80	xià	下	1:37	yán	言	1:51
shuǐ	水	1:91				xiān	仙	3:124		炎	1:122
shuì	税	1:144	wāi	歪	2:101		先	3:78		岩	3:123
	睡	3:94	wài	外	3:55		鲜	1:115	yàn	燕	2:99
shuō	说	1:64	wán	完	2:34	xian	线	2:135	yáng	羊	1:114
sī	丝	2:134	wàn	万	2:106		羡	1:120		洋	1:119
	私	2:133	wáng	王	3:1		现	3:4	yào	药	2:147
	思	3:97	wǎng	网	2:140	xiāng	香	1:150	yě	也	1:45
sū	苏	1:146	wàng	忘	1:174	xiǎng	想	1:172	yè	叶	1:133
suàn	算	1:139	wéi	维	2:144	xiàng	象	2:77		夜	3:57
suǒ	所	2:19	wèi				像	2:78	yī	衣	3:41
			or wéi	为	2:116	xiǎo	小	1:19		医	2:47
tā	他	1:46	wěi	尾	2:112	xiào	笑	1:140	yǐ	蚁	2:125
tài	太	1:17	wèi	未	1:168	xié	协	3:74		椅	3:86
tān	贪	2:9		胃	3:96	xiě	写	2:149	yì	义	1:118
tán	谈	1:123	wén	闻	2:28	xīn	心	1:69		忆	1:173
téng	疼	3:89		问	2:27		新	2:24		易	2:107
tǐ	体	1:163	wǒ	我	1:43	xìn	信	1:52		逸	2:82
tì	剃	2:42	wū	乌	1:106	xíng	行	3:62		意	1:173
tiān	天	1:15		屋	2:103	xìng	姓	1:85	yīn	因	2:4
tián	田	1:22				xiōng	兄	1:61	yín	银	2:11
	甜	3:103	xī	夕	3:51		凶	3:119	yǐn	引	2:39
tīng	听	3:105		西	1:35	xióng	熊	2:79		饮	3:20
tóu	头	2:123	xí	习	1:109	xiū	休	1:33	yìn	印	2:150
tū	凸	3:140	xǐ	洗	3:79	xū	须	2:122	yīng	英	1:136
	秃	1:145		喜	3:107	xué	学	1:98	yǒng	永	1:92
	突	2:56	xì	细	2:141	xuě	雪	2:148	yǒu	犹	2:58
tú	徒	3:65				xún	驯	2:67	yǒu	有	1:160

	友	1:40	yuè	乐	2:146		只	2:87	zhù	住	3:8
yòu	右	1:55	yún	云	1:97		枝	3:85	zhuāng	妆	3:49
yú	鱼	1:111				zhǐ	止	1:74		装	3:50
	渔	1:112	zá	杂	2:93		纸	2:139	zhuàng	壮	3:49
yǔ	羽	1:108	zāi	灾	1:125	zhì	至	2:102	zǐ	子	1:2
	雨	1:95	zǎo	早	1:32		质	2:23	zì	字	1:5
	语	3:137	zhǎn	斩	3:26	zhōng	中	1:38		自	1:72
yù	玉	3:2	zhǎo	爪	2:115		终	2:143	zǒu	走	1:80
	狱	2:52	zhēn	针	2:13	zhòng	众	3:134	zú	足	1:75
yuān	冤	2:81	zhēng	争	2:117	zhǒu	帚	3:34	zuì	醉	2:46
yuán	圆	3:130	zhèng	正	1:78	zhū	猪	1:6	zuǒ	左	1:54
yuàn	怨	3:60		政	3:101	zhú	竹	1:137	zuò	坐	1:82
yuē	月	1:26	zhī	知	2:44	zhǔ	主	3:7		做	3:133